THE PENGUIN POETS

KIPLING

Rudyard Kipling, son of John Lockwood Kipling, the author of *Beast and Man in India*, was born in Bombay in 1865. He was educated at the United Services College, Westward Ho!, and was engaged in journalistic work in India from 1882 to 1889. His fame rests principally on his short stories, dealing with India, the sea, the jungle and its beasts, the army, the navy, and a multitude of other subjects. His verse, as varied in subject as his prose, also enjoyed great popularity. Among his more famous publications are *Plain Tales from the Hills* (1888), *Life's Handicap* (1891), *Barrack-Room Ballads* (1892), *Kim* (1901), *Just So Stories* (1902), *Puck of Pook's Hill* (1906), and *Rewards and Fairies* (1910). Kipling, who was awarded a Nobel Prize in 1907, died in 1936.

KIPLING

A Selection by

JAMES COCHRANE

PENGUIN BOOKS

Penguin Books Ltd, Harmondsworth, Middlesex, England
Penguin Books, 625 Madison Avenue, New York, New York 10022, U.S.A.
Penguin Books Australia Ltd, Ringwood, Victoria, Australia
Penguin Books Canada Ltd, 2801 John Street, Markham, Ontario, Canada L3R 1B4
Penguin Books (N.Z.) Ltd, 182–190 Wairau Road, Auckland 10, New Zealand

—

First published 1977
Reprinted 1981

—

—

Set, printed and bound in Great Britain by
Cox & Wyman Ltd, Reading
Set in Monotype Caslon

CONTENTS

THE OVERLAND MAIL 11

ARITHMETIC ON THE FRONTIER 13

THE BETROTHED 15

ONE VICEROY RESIGNS 18

THE GALLEY-SLAVE 24

A TALE OF TWO CITIES 26

TWO MONTHS 29

L'ENVOI 31

DEDICATION FROM *Barrack-Room Ballads* 32

SESTINA OF THE TRAMP-ROYAL 34

ZION 36

THE SEA-WIFE 38

THE BROKEN MEN 40

GETHSEMANE 43

THE SONG OF THE BANJO 44

THE SEA AND THE HILLS 48

THE RHYME OF THE THREE SEALERS 50

MCANDREW'S HYMN 58

THE SECOND VOYAGE 65

THE FIRST CHANTEY 67
THE EXILES' LINE 69
THE LONG TRAIL 72
A SONG OF THE ENGLISH 76
OUR LADY OF THE SNOWS 86
RHODES MEMORIAL, TABLE MOUNTAIN 88
SUSSEX 89
THE VAMPIRE 93
THE ENGLISH FLAG 95
WHEN EARTH'S LAST PICTURE IS PAINTED 98
THE BALLAD OF EAST AND WEST 99
THE BALLAD OF BOH DA THONE 104
THE LESSON 114
THE ISLANDERS 116
THE DYKES 120
'THE CITY OF BRASS' 123
THE OLD MEN 126
THE WHITE MAN'S BURDEN 128
RECESSIONAL 130
'FOR ALL WE HAVE AND ARE' 132
THE THREE-DECKER 134

THE RHYME OF THE THREE CAPTAINS 136
THE CONUNDRUM OF THE WORKSHOPS 141
IN THE NEOLITHIC AGE 143
'WHEN 'OMER SMOTE 'IS BLOOMIN' LYRE' 145
THE FEMALE OF THE SPECIES 146
THE EXPLANATION 149
THE KING 150
THE SONS OF MARTHA 152
'BOBS' 155
DANNY DEEVER 158
TOMMY 160
'FUZZY-WUZZY' 162
CELLS 164
GUNGA DIN 166
THE WIDOW AT WINDSOR 169
BELTS 171
MANDALAY 173
TROOPIN' 175
FORD O' KABUL RIVER 177
GENTLEMEN-RANKERS 179
'BACK TO THE ARMY AGAIN' 181

'BIRDS OF PREY' MARCH 184
'SOLDIER AN' SAILOR TOO' 186
'THE MEN THAT FOUGHT AT MINDEN' 189
CHOLERA CAMP 191
THE LADIES 193
THE MOTHER-LODGE 196
'FOLLOW ME 'OME' 199
THE SERGEANT'S WEDDIN' 201
THE 'EATHEN 203
'MARY, PITY WOMEN!' 206
'FOR TO ADMIRE' 208
THE ABSENT-MINDED BEGGAR 210
CHANT-PAGAN 212
BOOTS 215
THE MARRIED MAN 217
LICHTENBERG 219
HALF-BALLADE OF WATERVAL 221
THE RETURN 223
'CITIES AND THRONES AND POWERS' 226
THE RECALL 227
PUCK'S SONG 228

THE WAY THROUGH THE WOODS 230
A CHARM 231
JOBSON'S AMEN 233
'MY NEW-CUT ASHLAR' 235
THE NEW KNIGHTHOOD 237
HARP SONG OF THE DANE WOMEN 239
THE PUZZLER 241
HADRAMAUTI 242
ROAD-SONG OF THE *Bandar-Log* 244
A PICT SONG 246
THE VOORTREKKER 248
A SCHOOL SONG 249
THE LAW OF THE JUNGLE 252
THE CHILDREN'S SONG 255
IF— 257
THE PRODIGAL SON 259
A TRANSLATION 261
OLD MOTHER LAIDINWOOL 262
THE LAND 264
JUST SO VERSES 267
THE LOOKING-GLASS 274

A SMUGGLER'S SONG 276

HERIOT'S FORD 278

SONG OF THE GALLEY-SLAVES 280

THE BEGINNINGS 281

THE IDIOT BOY 282

NORMAN AND SAXON 283

THE SECRET OF THE MACHINES 285

THE MASTER-COOK 287

WE AND THEY 289

THE LAST ODE 291

THE DISCIPLE 292

THE GODS OF THE COPYBOOK HEADINGS 294

THE CLERKS AND THE BELLS 297

'HIS APOLOGIES' 299

THE STORM CONE 301

THE APPEAL 302

INDEX OF TITLES 305

INDEX OF FIRST LINES 309

THE OVERLAND MAIL
(Foot-service to the Hills)

In the Name of the Empress of India, make way,
  O Lords of the Jungle, wherever you roam,
The woods are astir at the close of the day –
  We exiles are waiting for letters from Home.
Let the robber retreat – let the tiger turn tail –
In the Name of the Empress, the Overland Mail!

With a jingle of bells as the dusk gathers in,
  He turns to the footpath that heads up the hill –
The bags on his back and a cloth round his chin,
  And, tucked in his waistbelt, the Post Office bill: –
'Despatched on this date, as received by the rail,
'*Per* runner, two bags of the Overland Mail.'

Is the torrent in spate? He must ford it or swim.
  Has the rain wrecked the road? He must climb by the cliff.
Does the tempest cry halt? What are tempests to him?
  The service admits not a 'but' or an 'if'.
While the breath's in his mouth, he must bear without fail,
In the Name of the Empress, the Overland Mail.

From aloe to rose-oak, from rose-oak to fir,
  From level to upland, from upland to crest,
From rice-field to rock-ridge, from rock-ridge to spur,
  Fly the soft-sandalled feet, strains the brawny, brown chest
From rail to ravine – to the peak from the vale –
Up, up through the night goes the Overland Mail.

There's a speck on the hillside, a dot on the road –
   A jingle of bells on the footpath below –
There's a scuffle above in the monkey's abode –
   The world is awake and the clouds are aglow.
For the great Sun himself must attend to the hail: –
'In the Name of the Empress, the Overland Mail!'

ARITHMETIC ON THE FRONTIER

A great and glorious thing it is
  To learn, for seven years or so,
The Lord knows what of that and this,
  Ere reckoned fit to face the foe –
The flying bullet down the Pass,
That whistles clear: 'All flesh is grass.'

Three hundred pounds per annum spent
  On making brain and body meeter
For all the murderous intent
  Comprised in 'villainous saltpetre'!
And after? – Ask the Yusufzaies
What comes of all our 'ologies.

A scrimmage in a Border Station –
  A canter down some dark defile –
Two thousand pounds of education
  Drops to a ten-rupee jezail –
The Crammer's boast, the Squadron's pride,
Shot like a rabbit in a ride!

No proposition Euclid wrote
  No formulae the text-books know,
Will turn the bullet from your coat,
  Or ward the tulwar's downward blow.
Strike hard who cares – shoot straight who can –
The odds are on the cheaper man.

One sword-knot stolen from the camp
  Will pay for all the school expenses

Of any Kurrum Valley scamp
   Who knows no word of moods and tenses,
But, being blessed with perfect sight,
Picks off our messmates left and right.

With home-bred hordes the hillsides teem.
   The troopships bring us one by one,
At vast expense of time and steam,
   To slay Afridis where they run.
The 'captives of our bow and spear'
Are cheap, alas! as we are dear.

THE BETROTHED

'You must choose between me and your cigar.' –
Breach of Promise Case, circa 1885.

Open the old cigar-box, get me a Cuba stout,
For things are running crossways, and Maggie and I are out.

We quarrelled about Havanas – we fought o'er a good cheroot,
And *I* know she is exacting, and she says I am a brute.

Open the old cigar-box – let me consider a space;
In the soft blue veil of the vapour musing on Maggie's face.

Maggie is pretty to look at – Maggie's a loving lass,
But the prettiest cheeks must wrinkle, the truest of loves must pass.

There's peace in a Larranaga, there's calm in a Henry Clay;
But the best cigar in an hour is finished and thrown away –

Thrown away for another as perfect and ripe and brown –
But I could not throw away Maggie for fear o' the talk o' the town!

Maggie, my wife at fifty – grey and dour and old –
With never another Maggie to purchase for love or gold!

And the light of Days that have Been the dark of the Days that Are,
And Love's torch stinking and stale, like the butt of a dead cigar –

The butt of a dead cigar you are bound to keep in your pocket –
With never a new one to light tho' it's charred and black to the
socket!

Open the old cigar-box – let me consider a while.
Here is a mild Manila – there is a wifely smile.

Which is the better portion – bondage bought with a ring,
Or a harem of dusky beauties, fifty tied in a string?

Counsellors cunning and silent – comforters true and tried,
And never a one of the fifty to sneer at a rival bride?

Thought in the early morning, solace in time of woes,
Peace in the hush of the twilight, balm ere my eyelids close,

This will the fifty give me, asking nought in return,
With only a *Suttee's* passion – to do their duty and burn.

This will the fifty give me. When they are spent and dead,
Five times other fifties shall be my servants instead.

The furrows of far-off Java, the isles of the Spanish Main,
When they hear my harem is empty will send me my brides again.

I will take no heed to their raiment, nor food for their mouths withal,
So long as the gulls are nesting, so long as the showers fall.

I will scent 'em with best vanilla, with tea will I temper their hides,
And the Moor and the Mormon shall envy who read of the tale of
my brides.

For Maggie has written a letter to give me my choice between
The wee little whimpering Love and the great god Nick o' Teen.

And I have been servant of Love for barely a twelvemonth clear,
But I have been Priest of Cabanas a matter of seven year;

And the gloom of my bachelor days is flecked with the cheery light
Of stumps that I burned to Friendship and Pleasure and Work and
  Fight.

And I turn my eyes to the future that Maggie and I must prove,
But the only light on the marshes is the Will-o'-the-Wisp of Love.

Will it see me safe through my journey or leave me bogged in the
  mire?
Since a puff of tobacco can cloud it, shall I follow the fitful fire?

Open the old cigar-box – let me consider anew –
Old friends, and who is Maggie that I should abandon *you*?

A million surplus Maggies are willing to bear the yoke;
And a woman is only a woman, but a good Cigar is a Smoke.

Light me another Cuba – I hold to my first-sworn vows.
If Maggie will have no rival, I'll have no Maggie for Spouse!

ONE VICEROY RESIGNS

LORD DUFFERIN TO LORD LANSDOWNE:–

So here's your Empire. No more wine, then? Good.
We'll clear the Aides and *khitmutgars* away.
(You'll know that fat old fellow with the knife –
He keeps the Name Book, talks in English, too,
And almost thinks himself the Government.)
O Youth, Youth, Youth! Forgive me, you're so young.
Forty from sixty – twenty years of work
And power to back the working. *Ay de mí!*
You want to know, you want to see, to touch
And, by your lights, to act. It's natural.
I wonder can I help you? Let me try.
You saw – what did you see from Bombay east?
Enough to frighten any one but me?
Neat that! It frightened Me in Eighty-Four!
You shouldn't take a man from Canada
And bid him smoke in powder-magazines;
Nor with a Reputation such as – Bah!
That ghost has haunted me for twenty years,
My Reputation now full-blown. Your fault!
Yours, with your stories of the strife at Home,
Who's up, who's down, who leads and who is led –
One reads so much, one hears so little here.
Well, now's your turn of exile. I go back
To Rome and leisure. All roads lead to Rome,
Or books – the refuge of the destitute.
When you . . . that brings me back to India. See!
  Start clear. I couldn't. Egypt served my turn.
You'll never plumb the Oriental mind,

And if you did, it isn't worth the toil.
Think of a sleek French priest in Canada;
Divide by twenty half-breeds. Multiply
By twice the Sphinx's silence. There's your East,
And you're as wise as ever. So am I.
  Accept on trust and work in darkness, strike
At venture, stumble forward, make your mark,
(It's chalk on granite) then thank God no flame
Leaps from the rock to shrivel mark and man.
I'm clear – my mark is made. Three months of drouth
Had ruined much. It rained and washed away
The specks that might have gathered on my Name.
I took a country twice the size of France,
And shuttered up one doorway in the North.
I stand by those. You'll find that both will pay,
I pledged my Name on both – they're yours to-night.
Hold to them – they hold fame enough for two.
I'm old, but I shall live till Burma pays.
Men there – *not* German traders – Crosthwaite knows –
You'll find it in my papers. For the North
Guns always – quietly – but always guns.
You've seen your Council? Yes, they'll try to rule,
And prize their Reputations. Have you met
A grim lay-reader with a taste for coins,
And faith in Sin most men withhold from God?
He's gone to England. Ripon knew his grip
And kicked. A Council always has its Hopes.
They look for nothing from the West but Death
Or Bath or Bournemouth. Here's their ground. They fight
Until the Middle Classes take them back,
One of ten millions plus a C. S. I.,
Or drop in harness. Legion of the Lost?
Not altogether. Earnest, narrow men,

But chiefly earnest, and they'll do your work,
And end by writing letters to the *Times*.
(Shall I write letters, answering Hunter – fawn
With Ripon on the Yorkshire grocers? Ugh!)
They have their Reputations. Look to one –
I work with him – the smallest of them all,
White-haired, red-faced, who sat the plunging horse
Out in the garden. He's your right-hand man,
And dreams of tilting Wolseley from the throne,
But while he dreams gives work we cannot buy;
He has his Reputation – wants the Lords
By way of Frontier Roads. Meantime, I think,
He values very much the hand that falls
Upon his shoulder at the Council table –
Hates cats and knows his business. *Which is yours.*
　Your business! Twice a hundred million souls.
Your business! I could tell you what I did
Some nights of Eighty-five, at Simla, worth
A Kingdom's ransom. When a big ship drives
God knows to what new reef, the man at the wheel
Prays with the passengers. They lose their lives.
Or rescued go their way; but he's no man
To take his trick at the wheel again. That's worse
Than drowning. Well, a galled Mashobra mule
(You'll see Mashobra) passed me on the Mall,
And I was – some fool's wife had ducked and bowed
To show the others I would stop and speak.
Then the mule fell – three galls, a hand-breadth each,
Behind the withers. Mrs. Whatsisname
Leers at the mule and me by turns, thweet thoul!
'How could they make him carry such a load!'
I saw – it isn't often I dream dreams –
More than the mule that minute – smoke and flame

From Simla to the haze below. That's weak.
You're younger. You'll dream dreams before you've done.
You've youth, that's one; good workmen – that means two
Fair chances in your favour. Fate's the third.
I know what *I* did. Do you ask me, 'Preach?'
I answer by my past or else go back
To platitudes of rule – or take you thus
In confidence and say: – 'You know the trick:
'You've governed Canada. You know. *You* know!'
And all the while commend you to Fate's hand
(Here at the top one loses sight o' God),
Commend you, then, to something more than you –
The Other People's blunders and . . . that's all.
I'd agonise to serve you if I could.
It's incommunicable, like the cast
That drops the hackle with the gut adry.
Too much – too little – there's your salmon lost!
And so I tell you nothing – wish you luck,
And wonder – how I wonder! – for your sake!
And triumph for my own. You're young, you're young,
You hold to half a hundred Shibboleths.
I'm old. I followed Power to the last,
Gave her my best, and Power followed Me.
It's worth it – on my soul I'm speaking plain,
Here by the claret glasses! – worth it all.
I gave – no matter what I gave – I win.
I *know* I win. Mine's work, good work that lives!
A country twice the size of France – the North
Safeguarded. That's my record: sink the rest
And better if you can. The Rains may serve,
Rupees may rise – threepence will give you Fame –
It's rash to hope for sixpence. If they rise
Get guns, more guns, and lift the salt-tax . . . Oh!

I told you what the Congress meant or thought?
I'll answer nothing. Half a year will prove
The full extent of time and thought you'll spare
To Congress. Ask a Lady Doctor *once*
How little Begums see the light – deduce
Thence how the True Reformer's child is born.
It's interesting, curious . . . and vile.
I told the Turk he was a gentleman.
I told the Russian that his Tartar veins
Bled pure Parisian ichor; and he purred.
The Congress doesn't purr. I think it swears.
You're young – you'll swear too ere you've reached the end.
The End! God help you, if there be a God.
(There must be one to startle Gladstone's soul
In that new land where all the wires are cut,
And Cross snores anthems on the asphodel.)
God help you! And I'd help you if I could,
But that's beyond me. Yes, your speech was crude.
Sound claret after olives – yours and mine;
But Médoc slips into vin ordinaire.
(I'll drink my first at Genoa to your health)
Raise it to Hock. You'll never catch my style.
And, after all, the middle-classes grip
The middle-class – for Brompton talk Earl's Court.
Perhaps you're right. I'll see you in the *Times* –
A quarter-column of eye-searing print,
A leader once a quarter – then a war;
The Strand a-bellow through the fog: – 'Defeat!'
''Orrible slaughter!' While you lie awake
And wonder. Oh, you'll wonder ere you're free!
I wonder now. The four years slide away
So fast, so fast, and leave me here alone.
Reay, Colvin, Lyall, Roberts, Buck, the rest,

Princes and Powers of Darkness, troops and trains,
(I *cannot* sleep in trains), land piled on land,
Whitewash and weariness, red rockets, dust,
White snows that mocked me, palaces – with draughts,
And Westland with the drafts he couldn't pay.
Poor Wilson reading his obituary
Before he died, and Hope, the man with bones,
And Aitchison a dripping mackintosh
At Council in the Rains, his grating 'Sirrr'
Half drowned by Hunter's silky: 'Bât, my lahd.'
Hunterian always: Marshal spinning plates
Or standing on his head; the Rent Bill's roar,
A hundred thousand speeches, much red cloth,
And Smiths thrice happy if I called them Jones,
(I can't remember half their names) or reined
My pony on the Mall to greet their wives.
More trains, more troops, more dust, and then all's done . . .
Four years, and I forget. If I forget,
How will *they* bear me in their minds? The North
Safeguarded – nearly (Roberts knows the rest),
A country twice the size of France annexed.
That stays at least. The rest may pass – may pass –
Your heritage – and I can teach you naught.
'High trust,' 'vast honour,' 'interests twice as vast,'
'Due reverence to your Council' – keep to those.
I envy you the twenty years you've gained,
But not the five to follow. What's that? One!
Two! – Surely not so late. Good-night. *Don't* dream.

THE GALLEY-SLAVE

Oh, gallant was our galley from her carven steering-wheel
To her figurehead of silver and her beak of hammered steel.
The leg-bar chafed the ankle and we gasped for cooler air,
But no galley on the waters with our galley could compare!

Our bulkheads bulged with cotton and our masts were stepped in gold –
We ran a mighty merchandise of niggers in the hold;
The white foam spun behind us, and the black shark swam below,
As we gripped the kicking sweep-head and we made the galley go.

It was merry in the galley, for we revelled now and then –
If they wore us down like cattle, faith, we fought and loved like men!
As we snatched her through the water, so we snatched a minute's bliss,
And the mutter of the dying never spoiled the lover's kiss.

Our women and our children toiled beside us in the dark –
They died, we filed their fetters, and we heaved them to the shark –
We heaved them to the fishes, but so fast the galley sped
We had only time to envy, for we could not mourn our dead.

Bear witness, once my comrades, what a hard-bit gang were we –
The servants of the sweep-head, but the masters of the sea!
By the hands that drove her forward as she plunged and yawed and sheered,
Woman, Man, or God or Devil, was there anything we feared?

Was it storm? Our fathers faced it and a wilder never blew.
Earth that waited for the wreckage watched the galley struggle through.

Burning noon or choking midnight, Sickness, Sorrow, Parting, Death?
Nay, our very babes would mock you had they time for idle breath.

But to-day I leave the galley and another takes my place;
There's my name upon the deck-beam – let it stand a little space.
I am free – to watch my messmates beating out to open main,
Free of all that Life can offer – save to handle sweep again.

By the brand upon my shoulder, by the gall of clinging steel,
By the welts the whips have left me, by the scars that never heal;
By eyes grown old with staring through the sunwash on the brine,
I am paid in full for service. Would that service still were mine!

Yet they talk of times and seasons and of woe the years bring forth,
Of our galley swamped and shattered in the rollers of the North;
When the niggers break the hatches and the decks are gay with gore,
And a craven-hearted pilot crams her crashing on the shore.

She will need no half-mast signal, minute-gun, or rocket-flare.
When the cry for help goes seaward, she will find her servants there.
Battered chain-gangs of the orlop, grizzled drafts of years gone by,
To the bench that broke their manhood, they shall lash themselves and die.

Hale and crippled, young and aged, paid, deserted, shipped away –
Palace, cot, and lazaretto shall make up the tale that day,
When the skies are black above them, and the decks ablaze beneath,
And the top-men clear the raffle with their clasp-knives in their teeth.

It may be that Fate will give me life and leave to row once more –
Set some strong man free for fighting as I take awhile his oar.
But to-day I leave the galley. Shall I curse her service then?
God be thanked! Whate'er comes after, I have lived and toiled with Men!

A TALE OF TWO CITIES

Where the sober-coloured cultivator smiles
On his *byles*;[1]
Where the cholera, the cyclone, and the crow
Come and go;
Where the merchant deals in indigo and tea,
Hides and *ghi*;[2]
Where the Babu drops inflammatory hints
In his prints;
Stands a City – Charnock chose it – packed away
Near a Bay –
By the sewage rendered fetid, by the sewer
Made impure,
By the Sunderbunds unwholesome, by the swamp
Moist and damp;
And the City and the Viceroy, as we see,
Don't agree.

Once, two hundred years ago, the trader came
Meek and tame.
Where his timid foot first halted, there he stayed,
Till mere trade
Grew to Empire, and he sent his armies forth
South and North,
Till the country from Peshawur to Ceylon
Was his own.
Thus the midday halt of Charnock – more's the pity! –
Grew a City.
As the fungus sprouts chaotic from its bed,
So it spread –

[1] Cattle. [2] Butter.

Chance-directed, chance-erected, laid and built
On the silt –
Palace, byre, hovel – poverty and pride –
Side by side;
And, above the packed and pestilential town,
Death looked down.

But the Rulers in that City by the Sea
Turned to flee –
Fled, with each returning Spring-tide, from its ills
To the Hills.
From the clammy fogs of morning, from the blaze
Of the days,
From the sickness of the noontide, from the heat,
Beat retreat;
For the country from Peshawur to Ceylon
Was their own.
But the Merchant risked the perils of the Plain
For his gain.

Now the resting-place of Charnock, 'neath the palms,
Asks an alms,
And the burden of its lamentation is,
Briefly, this: –
'Because, for certain months, we boil and stew,
'So should you.
'Cast the Viceroy and his Council, to perspire
'In our fire!'
And for answer to the argument, in vain
We explain
That an amateur Saint Lawrence cannot cry: —
'*All* must fry!'
That the Merchant risks the perils of the Plains
For his gains.

Nor can Rulers rule a house that men grow rich in,
From its kitchen.

Let the Babu drop inflammatory hints
In his prints;
And mature – consistent soul – his plan for stealing
To Darjeeling:
Let the Merchant seek, who makes his silver pile,
England's isle;
Let the City Charnock pitched on – evil day! –
Go Her way.
Though the argosies of Asia at Her doors
Heap their stores,
Though Her enterprise and energy secure
Income sure,
Though 'out-station orders punctually obeyed'
Swell Her trade –
Still, for rule, administration, and the rest,
Simla's best![1]

[1] *Simla*: Summer residence of the Viceroy and of those other Europeans who were able to retire to the Hills. (Ed.)

TWO MONTHS

JUNE

No hope, no change! The clouds have shut us in,
   And through the cloud the sullen Sun strikes down
   Full on the bosom of the tortured Town,
Till Night falls heavy as remembered sin
That will not suffer sleep or thought of ease,
   And, hour on hour, the dry-eyed Moon in spite
   Glares through the haze and mocks with watery light
The torment of the uncomplaining trees.
Far off, the Thunder bellows her despair
To echoing Earth, thrice parched. The lightnings fly
In vain. No help the heaped-up clouds afford,
But wearier weight of burdened, burning air.
What truce with Dawn? Look, from the aching sky,
Day stalks, a tyrant with a flaming sword!

SEPTEMBER

At dawn there was a murmur in the trees,
   A ripple on the tank, and in the air
   Presage of coming coolness – everywhere
A voice of prophecy upon the breeze.
Up leapt the Sun and smote the dust to gold,
   And strove to parch anew the heedless land,
All impotently, as a King grown old
   Wars for the Empire crumbling 'neath his hand.
   One after one the lotos-petals fell,
   Beneath the onslaught of the rebel year,
   In mutiny against a furious sky;

And far-off Winter whispered: – 'It is well!
'Hot Summer dies. Behold your help is near,
'For when men's need is sorest, then come I.'

L'ENVOI
(Departmental Ditties)

The smoke upon your Altar dies,
The flowers decay,
The Goddess of your sacrifice
Has flown away.
What profit then to sing or slay
The sacrifice from day to day?

'We know the Shrine is void,' they said,
'The Goddess flown –
'Yet wreaths are on the altar laid -
'The Altar-Stone
'Is black with fumes of sacrifice,
'Albeit She has fled our eyes.

'For, it may be, if still we sing
'And tend the Shrine,
'Some Deity on wandering wing
'May there incline;
'And, finding all in order meet,
'Stay while we worship at Her feet.'

DEDICATION FROM *BARRACK-ROOM BALLADS*

Beyond the path of the outmost sun through utter darkness hurled –
Farther than ever comet flared or vagrant star-dust swirled –
Live such as fought and sailed and ruled and loved and made our world.

They are purged of pride because they died; they know the worth of their bays;
They sit at wine with the Maidens Nine and the Gods of the Elder Days –
It is their will to serve or be still as fitteth Our Father's praise.

'Tis theirs to sweep through the ringing deep where Azrael's outposts are,
Or buffet a path through the Pit's red wrath when God goes out to war,
Or hang with the reckless Seraphim on the rein of a red-maned star.

They take their mirth in the joy of the Earth – they dare not grieve for her pain.
They know of toil and the end of toil; they know God's Law is plain;
So they whistle the Devil to make them sport who know that Sin is vain.

And oft-times cometh our wise Lord God, master of every trade,
And tells them tales of His daily toil, of Edens newly made;
And they rise to their feet as He passes by, gentlemen unafraid.

To these who are cleansed of base Desire, Sorrow and Lust and Shame –

Gods for they knew the hearts of men, men for they stooped to
Fame –
Borne on the breath that men call Death, my brother's spirit came.

He scarce had need to doff his pride or slough the dross of Earth –
E'en as he trod that day to God so walked he from his birth,
In simpleness and gentleness and honour and clean mirth.

So cup to lip in fellowship they gave him welcome high
And made him place at the banquet board – the Strong Men ranged
thereby,
Who had done his work and held his peace and had no fear to die.

Beyond the loom of the last lone star, through open darkness hurled,
Further than rebel comet dared or hiving star-swarm swirled,
Sits he with those that praise our God for that they served His world.

SESTINA OF THE TRAMP-ROYAL

1896

Speakin' in general, I 'ave tried 'em all –
The 'appy roads that take you o'er the world.
Speakin' in general, I 'ave found them good
For such as cannot use one bed too long,
But must get 'ence, the same as I 'ave done,
An' go observin' matters till they die.

What do it matter where or 'ow we die,
So long as we've our 'ealth to watch it all –
The different ways that different things are done,
An' men an' women lovin' in this world;
Takin' our chances as they come along,
An' when they ain't, pretendin' they are good?

In cash or credit – no, it aren't no good;
You 'ave to 'ave the 'abit or you'd die,
Unless you lived your life but one day long,
Nor didn't prophesy nor fret at all,
But drew your tucker some'ow from the world,
An' never bothered what you might ha' done.

But, Gawd, what things are they I 'aven't done?
I've turned my 'and to most, an' turned it good,
In various situations round the world –
For 'im that doth not work must surely die;
But that's no reason man should labour all
'Is life on one same shift – life's none so long.

Therefore, from job to job I've moved along.
Pay couldn't 'old me when my time was done,
For something in my 'ead upset it all,
Till I 'ad dropped whatever 'twas for good,
An', out at sea, be'eld the dock-lights die,
An' met my mate – the wind that tramps the world!

It's like a book, I think, this bloomin' world,
Which you can read and care for just so long,
But presently you feel that you will die
Unless you get the page you're readin' done,
An' turn another – likely not so good;
But what you're after is to turn 'em all.

Gawd bless this world! Whatever she 'ath done –
Excep' when awful long – I've found it good.
So write, before I die, ''E liked it all!'

ZION
1914–18

The Doorkeepers of Zion,
  They do not always stand
In helmet and whole armour,
  With halberds in their hand;
But, being sure of Zion,
  And all her mysteries,
They rest awhile in Zion,
Sit down and smile in Zion;
Ay, even jest in Zion;
  In Zion, at their ease.

The Gatekeepers of Baal,
  They dare not sit or lean,
But fume and fret and posture
  And foam and curse between;
For, being bound to Baal,
  Whose sacrifice is vain,
Their rest is scant with Baal,
They glare and pant for Baal,
They mouth and rant for Baal;
  For Baal in their pain.

But we will go to Zion,
  By choice and not through dread,
With these our present comrades
  And those our present dead;
And, being free of Zion
  In both her fellowships,

ZION

Sit down and sup in Zion –
Stand up and drink in Zion
Whatever cup in Zion
　Is offered to our lips!

THE SEA-WIFE
1893

There dwells a wife by the Northern Gate,
  And a wealthy wife is she;
She breeds a breed of roving men
  And casts them over sea.

And some are drowned in deep water,
  And some in sight o' shore,
And word goes back to the weary wife
  And ever she sends more.

For since that wife had gate or gear,
  Or hearth or garth or field,
She willed her sons to the white harvest,
  And that is a bitter yield.

She wills her sons to the wet ploughing,
  To ride the horse of tree;
And syne her sons come back again
  Far-spent from out the sea.

The good wife's sons come home again
  With little into their hands,
But the lore of men that have dealt with men
  In the new and naked lands;

But the faith of men that have brothered men
  By more than easy breath,
And the eyes of men that have read with men
  In the open books of Death.

Rich are they, rich in wonders seen,
  But poor in the goods of men;
So what they have got by the skin of their teeth
  They sell for their teeth again.

And whether they lose to the naked life
  Or win to their hearts' desire,
They tell it all to the weary wife
  That nods beside the fire.

Her hearth is wide to every wind
  That makes the white ash spin;
And tide and tide and 'tween the tides
  Her sons go out and in;

(Out with great mirth that do desire
  Hazard of trackless ways –
In with content to wait their watch
  And warm before the blaze);

And some return by failing light,
  And some in waking dream,
For she hears the heels of the dripping ghosts
  That ride the rough roof-beam.

Home, they come home from all the ports,
  The living and the dead;
The good wife's sons come home again
  For her blessing on their head!

THE BROKEN MEN
1902

For things we never mention,
  For Art misunderstood –
For excellent intention
  That did not turn to good;
From ancient tales' renewing,
  From clouds we would not clear –
Beyond the Law's pursuing
  We fled, and settled here.

We took no tearful leaving,
  We bade no long good-byes.
Men talked of crime and thieving,
  Men wrote of fraud and lies.
To save our injured feelings
  'Twas time and time to go –
Behind was dock and Dartmoor,
  Ahead lay Callao!

The widow and the orphan
  That pray for ten per cent,
They clapped their trailers on us
  To spy the road we went.
They watched the foreign sailings
  (They scan the shipping still),
And that's your Christian people
  Returning good for ill!

God bless the thoughtful islands
  Where never warrants come;

God bless the just Republics
  That give a man a home,
That ask no foolish questions,
  But set him on his feet;
And save his wife and daughters
  From the workhouse and the street!

On church and square and market
  The noonday silence falls;
You'll hear the drowsy mutter
  Of the fountain in our halls.
Asleep amid the yuccas
  The city takes her ease –
Till twilight brings the land-wind
  To the clicking jalousies.

Day long the diamond weather,
  The high, unaltered blue –
The smell of goats and incense
  And the mule-bells tinkling through.
Day long the warder ocean
  That keeps us from our kin,
And once a month our levée
  When the English mail comes in.

You'll find us up and waiting
  To treat you at the bar;
You'll find us less exclusive
  Than the average English are.
We'll meet you with a carriage,
  Too glad to show you round,
But – we do not lunch on steamers,
  For they are English ground.

We sail o' nights to England
  And join our smiling Boards –
Our wives go in with Viscounts
  And our daughters dance with Lords,
But behind our princely doings,
  And behind each coup we make,
We feel there's Something Waiting,
  And – we meet It when we wake.

Ah, God! One sniff of England –
  To greet our flesh and blood –
To hear the traffic slurring
  Once more through London mud!
Our towns of wasted honour –
  Our streets of lost delight!
How stands the old Lord Warden?
  Are Dover's cliffs still white?

GETHSEMANE
1914–18

The Garden called Gethsemane
  In Picardy it was,
And there the people came to see
  The English soldiers pass.
We used to pass – we used to pass
  Or halt, as it might be,
And ship our masks in case of gas
  Beyond Gethsemane.

The Garden called Gethsemane,
  It held a pretty lass,
But all the time she talked to me
  I prayed my cup might pass.
The officer sat on the chair,
  The men lay on the grass,
And all the time we halted there
  I prayed my cup might pass.

It didn't pass – it didn't pass –
  It didn't pass from me.
I drank it when we met the gas
  Beyond Gethsemane!

THE SONG OF THE BANJO
1894

You couldn't pack a Broadwood half a mile –
  You mustn't leave a fiddle in the damp –
You couldn't raft an organ up the Nile,
  And play it in an Equatorial swamp.
I travel with the cooking-pots and pails –
  I'm sandwiched 'tween the coffee and the pork –
And when the dusty column checks and tails,
  You should hear me spur the rearguard to a walk!

  With my '*Pilly-willy-winky-winky-popp!*'
    (Oh, it's any tune that comes into my head!)
  So I keep 'em moving forward till they drop;
    So I play 'em up to water and to bed.

In the silence of the camp before the fight,
  When it's good to make your will and say your prayer,
You can hear my *strumpty-tumpty* overnight,
  Explaining ten to one was always fair.
I'm the Prophet of the Utterly Absurd,
  Of the Patently Impossible and Vain –
And when the Thing that Couldn't has occurred
  Give me time to change my leg and go again.

  With my '*Tumpa-tumpa-tumpa-tumpa-tump!*'
    In the desert where the dung-fed camp-smoke curled.
  There was never voice before us till I led our lonely chorus,
    I – the war-drum of the White Man round the world!

By the bitter road the Younger Son must tread,
  Ere he win to hearth and saddle of his own, –

'Mid the riot of the shearers at the shed,
  In the silence of the herder's hut alone –
In the twilight, on a bucket upside down,
  Hear me babble what the weakest won't confess –
I am Memory and Torment – I am Town!
  I am all that ever went with evening dress!

  With my '*Tunka-tunka-tunka-tunka-tunk!*'
    (So the lights – the London Lights – grow near and plain!)
  So I rowel 'em afresh towards the Devil and the Flesh,
    Till I bring my broken rankers home again.

In desire of many marvels over sea,
  Where the new-raised tropic city sweats and roars,
I have sailed with Young Ulysses from the quay
  Till the anchor rumbled down on stranger shores.
He is blooded to the open and the sky,
  He is taken in a snare that shall not fail,
He shall hear me singing strongly, till he die,
  Like the shouting of a backstay in a gale.

With my '*Hya! Heeya! Heeya! Hullah! Haul!*'
  (Oh, the green that thunders aft along the deck!)
Are you sick o' towns and men? You must sign and sail again,
  For it's 'Johnny Bowlegs, pack your kit and trek!'

Through the gorge that gives the stars at noon-day clear –
  Up the pass that packs the scud beneath our wheel –
Round the bluff that sinks her thousand fathom sheer –
  Down the valley with our guttering brakes asqueal:
Where the trestle groans and quivers in the snow,
  Where the many-shedded levels loop and twine,
Hear me lead my reckless children from below
  Till we sing the Song of Roland to the pine!

With my '*Tinka-tinka-tinka-tinka-tink!*'
(Oh, the axe has cleared the mountain, croup and crest!)
And we ride the iron stallions down to drink,
Through the cañons to the waters of the West!

And the tunes that mean so much to you alone –
Common tunes that make you choke and blow your nose –
Vulgar tunes that bring the laugh that brings the groan –
I can rip your very heartstrings out with those;
With the feasting, and the folly, and the fun –
And the lying, and the lusting, and the drink,
And the merry play that drops you, when you're done,
To the thoughts that burn like irons if you think.

With my '*Plunka-lunka-lunka-lunka-lunk!*'
Here's a trifle on account of pleasure past,
Ere the wit that made you win gives you eyes to see your sin
And – the heavier repentance at the last!

Let the organ moan her sorrow to the roof –
I have told the naked stars the Grief of Man!
Let the trumpet snare the foeman to the proof –
I have known Defeat, and mocked it as we ran!
My bray ye may not alter nor mistake
When I stand to jeer the fatted Soul of Things,
But the Song of Lost Endeavour that I make,
Is it hidden in the twanging of the strings?

With my '*Ta-ra-rara-rara-ra-ra-rrrp!*'
(Is it naught to you that hear and pass me by?)
But the word – the word is mine, when the order moves the line
And the lean, locked ranks go roaring down to die!

The grandam of my grandam was the Lyre –
(Oh, the blue below the little fisher-huts!)

That the Stealer stooping beachward filled with fire,
  Till she bore my iron head and ringing guts!
By the wisdom of the centuries I speak –
  To the tune of yestermorn I set the truth –
I, the joy of life unquestioned – I, the Greek –
  I, the everlasting Wonder-song of Youth!

With my '*Tinka-tinka-tinka-tinka-tink!*'
  (What d'ye lack, my noble masters! What d'ye lack?)
So I draw the world together link by link:
  Yea, from Delos up to Limerick and back!

THE SEA AND THE HILLS
1902

Who hath desired the Sea? – the sight of salt water unbounded –
The heave and the halt and the hurl and the crash of the comber
  wind-hounded?
The sleek-barrelled swell before storm, grey, foamless, enormous,
  and growing –
Stark calm on the lap of the Line or the crazy-eyed hurricane
  blowing –
His Sea in no showing the same – his Sea and the same 'neath each
  showing:
    His Sea as she slackens or thrills?
So and no otherwise – so and no otherwise – hillmen desire their
  Hills!

Who hath desired the Sea? – the immense and contemptuous surges?
The shudder, the stumble, the swerve, as the star-stabbing bowsprit
  emerges?
The orderly clouds of the Trades, the ridged, roaring sapphire
  thereunder –
Unheralded cliff-haunting flaws and the headsail's low-volleying
  thunder –
His Sea in no wonder the same – his Sea and the same through each
  wonder:
    His Sea as she rages or stills?
So and no otherwise – so and no otherwise – hillmen desire their
  Hills.

Who hath desired the Sea? Her menaces swift as her mercies?
The in-rolling walls of the fog and the silver-winged breeze that
  disperses?

The unstable mined berg going South and the calvings and groans
that declare it –
White water half-guessed overside and the moon breaking timely to
bare it –
His Sea as his fathers have dared – his Sea as his children shall dare it:
His Sea as she serves him or kills?
So and no otherwise – so and no otherwise – hillmen desire their
Hills.

Who hath desired the Sea? Her excellent loneliness rather
Than forecourts of kings, and her outermost pits than the streets
where men gather
Inland, among dust, under trees – inland where the slayer may slay
him –
Inland, out of reach of her arms, and the bosom whereon he must lay
him –
His Sea from the first that betrayed – at the last that shall never
betray him:
His Sea that his being fulfils?
So and no otherwise – so and no otherwise – hillmen desire their
Hills.

THE RHYME OF THE THREE SEALERS
1893

Away by the lands of the Japanee
Where the paper lanterns glow
And the crews of all the shipping drink
In the house of Blood Street Joe,
At twilight, when the landward breeze
Brings up the harbour noise,
And ebb of Yokohama Bay
Swigs chattering through the buoys,
In Cisco's Dewdrop Dining Rooms
They tell the tale anew
Of a hidden sea and a hidden fight,
When the Baltic *ran from the* Northern Light,
And the Stralsund *fought the two.*

Now this is the Law of the Muscovite, that he proves with shot and steel,
When you come by his isles in the Smoky Sea you must not take the seal,
Where the grey sea goes nakedly between the weed-hung shelves,
And the little blue fox he is bred for his skin and the seal they breed for themselves.
For when the *matkas*[1] seek the shore to drop their pups aland,
The great man-seal haul out of the sea, aroaring, band by band.
And when the first September gales have slaked their rutting wrath,
The great man-seal haul back to the sea and no man knows their path.
Then dark they lie and stark they lie – rookery, dune, and floe,
And the Northern Lights come down o' nights to dance with the houseless snow;

[1] She-seals.

And God Who clears the grounding berg and steers the grinding floe,
He hears the cry of the little kit-fox and the wind along the snow.
But since our women must walk gay and money buys their gear,
The sealing-boats they filch that way at hazard year by year.
English they be and Japanee that hang on the Brown Bear's flank,
And some be Scot, but the worst of the lot, and the boldest thieves, be Yank!

It was the sealer *Northern Light*, to the Smoky Seas she bore,
With a stovepipe stuck from a starboard port and the Russian flag at her fore.
(*Baltic*, *Stralsund*, and *Northern Light* – oh! they were birds of a feather –
Slipping away to the Smoky Seas, three seal-thieves together!)
And at last she came to a sandy cove and the *Baltic* lay therein,
But her men were up with the herding seal to drive and club and skin.
There were fifteen hundred skins abeach, cool pelt and proper fur,
When the *Northern Light* drove into the bight and the sea-mist drove with her.
The *Baltic* called her men and weighed – she could not choose but run –
For a stovepipe seen through the closing mist, it shows like a four-inch gun
(And loss it is that is sad as death to lose both trip and ship
And lie for a rotting contraband on Vladivostok slip).
She turned and dived in the sea-smother as a rabbit dives in the whins,
And the *Northern Light* sent up her boats to steal the stolen skins.
They had not brought a load to side or slid their hatches clear,
When they were aware of a sloop-of-war, ghost-white and very near.

Her flag she showed, and her guns she showed – three of them, black, abeam,
And a funnel white with the crusted salt, but never a show of steam.

There was no time to man the brakes, they knocked the shackle free,
And the *Northern Light* stood out again, goose-winged to open sea.
(For life it is that is worse than death, by force of Russian law,
To work in the mines of mercury that loose the teeth in your jaw.)
They had not run a mile from shore – they heard no shots behind –
When the skipper smote his hand on his thigh and threw her up in the wind:
'Bluffed – raised out on a bluff,' said he, 'for if my name's Tom Hall,
'You must set a thief to catch a thief – and a thief has caught us all!
'By every butt in Oregon and every spar in Maine,
'The hand that spilled the wind from her sail was the hand of Reuben Paine!
'He has rigged and trigged her with paint and spar, and, faith, he has faked her well –
'But I'd know the *Stralsund's* deckhouse yet from here to the booms o' Hell.
'Oh, once we ha' met at Baltimore, and twice on Boston pier,
'But the sickest day for you, Reuben Paine, was the day that you came here –
'The day that you came here, my lad, to scare us from our seal
'With your funnel made o' your painted cloth, and your guns o' rotten deal!
'Ring and blow for the *Baltic* now, and head her back to the bay,
'And we'll come into the game again – with a double deck to play!'

They rang and blew the sealers' call – the poaching-cry of the sea –
And they raised the *Baltic* out of the mist, and an angry ship was she.

And blind they groped through the whirling white and blind to the bay again,
Till they heard the creak of the *Stralsund's* boom and the clank of her mooring chain.
They laid them down by bitt and boat, their pistols in their belts,
And: 'Will you fight for it, Reuben Paine, or will you share the pelts?'

A dog-toothed laugh laughed Reuben Paine, and bared his flenching-knife.
'Yea, skin for skin, and all that he hath a man will give for his life;
'But I've six thousand skins below, and Yeddo Port to see,
'And there's never a law of God or man runs north of Fifty-Three:
'So go in peace to the naked seas with empty holds to fill,
'And I'll be good to your seal this catch, as many as I shall kill!'

Answered the snap of a closing lock – the jar of a gun-butt slid,
But the tender fog shut fold on fold to hide the wrong they did.
The weeping fog rolled fold on fold the wrath of man to cloak,
As the flame-spurts pale ran down the rail and the sealing-rifles spoke.
The bullets bit on bend and butt, the splinter slivered free
(Little they trust to sparrow-dust that stop the seal in his sea!),
The thick smoke hung and would not shift, leaden it lay and blue,
But three were down on the *Baltic's* deck and two of the *Stralsund's* crew.
An arm's length out and overside the banked fog held them bound,
But, as they heard or groan or word, they fired at the sound.
For one cried out on the Name of God, and one to have him cease,
And the questing volley found them both and bade them hold their peace.
And one called out on a heathen joss and one on the Virgin's Name,
And the schooling bullet leaped across and led them whence they came.

And in the waiting silences the rudder whined beneath,
And each man drew his watchful breath slow-taken 'tween the teeth –
Trigger and ear and eye acock, knit brow and hard-drawn lips –
Bracing his feet by chock and cleat for the rolling of the ships.
Till they heard the cough of a wounded man that fought in the fog for breath,
Till they heard the torment of Reuben Paine that wailed upon his death:

'The tides they'll go through Fundy Race, but I'll go never more
'And see the hogs from ebb-tide mark turn scampering back to shore.
'No more I'll see the trawlers drift below the Bass Rock ground,
'Or watch the tall Fall steamer lights tear blazing up the Sound.
'Sorrow is me, in a lonely sea and a sinful fight I fall,
'But if there's law o' God or man you'll swing for it yet, Tom Hall!'

Tom Hall stood up by the quarter-rail. 'Your words in your teeth,' said he.
'There's never a law of God or man runs north of Fifty-Three.
'So go in grace with Him to face, and an ill-spent life behind,
'And I'll be good to your widows, Rube, as many as I shall find.'
A *Stralsund* man shot blind and large, and a warlock Finn was he,
And he hit Tom Hall with a bursting ball a hand's-breadth over the knee.
Tom Hall caught hold by the topping-lift, and sat him down with an oath,
'You'll wait a little, Rube,' he said, 'the Devil has called for both.
'The Devil is driving both this tide, and the killing-grounds are close,
'And we'll go up to the Wrath of God as the holluschickie[1] goes.
'O men, put back your guns again and lay your rifles by,

[1] The young seal.

'We've fought our fight, and the best are down. Let up and let us die!
'Quit firing, by the bow there – quit! Call off the *Baltic's* crew!
'You're sure of Hell as me or Rube – but wait till we get through.'

There went no word between the ships, but thick and quick and loud
The life-blood drummed on the dripping decks, with the fog-dew from the shroud.
The sea-pull drew them side by side, gunnel to gunnel laid,
And they felt the sheer-strakes pound and clear, but never a word was said.

Then Reuben Paine cried out again before his spirit passed:
'Have I followed the sea for thirty years to die in the dark at last?
'Curse on her work that has nipped me here with a shifty trick unkind –
'I have gotten my death where I got my bread, but I dare not face it blind.
'Curse on the fog! Is there never a wind of all the winds I knew
'To clear the smother from off my chest, and let me look at the blue?'
The good fog heard – like a splitten sail, to left and right she tore,
And they saw the sun-dogs in the haze and the seal upon the shore.
Silver and grey ran spit and bay to meet the steel-backed tide,
And pinched and white in the clearing light the crews stared overside.
O rainbow-gay the red pools lay that swilled and spilled and spread,
And gold, raw gold, the spent shells rolled between the careless dead –
The dead that rocked so drunkenwise to weather and to lee,
And they saw the work their hands had done as God had bade them see!

And a little breeze blew over the rail that made the headsails lift,
But no man stood by wheel or sheet, and they let the schooners drift.

And the rattle rose in Reuben's throat and he cast his soul with a cry,
And 'Gone already?' Tom Hall he said. 'Then it's time for me to
die.'
His eyes were heavy with great sleep and yearning for the land,
And he spoke as a man that talks in dreams, his wound beneath his
hand.

'Oh, there comes no good o' the westering wind that backs against
the sun;
'Wash down the decks – they're all too red – and share the skins and
run.
Baltic, *Stralsund*, and *Northern Light* – clean share and share for all,
'You'll find the fleets off Tolstoi Mees, but you will not find Tom
Hall.
'Evil he did in shoal-water and blacker sin on the deep,
'But now he's sick of watch and trick and now he'll turn and sleep.
'He'll have no more of the crawling sea that made him suffer so,
'But he'll lie down on the killing-grounds where the holluschickie go.
'And west you'll sail and south again, beyond the sea-fog's rim,
'And tell the Yoshiwara girls to burn a stick for him.
'And you'll not weight him by the heels and dump him overside,
'But carry him up to the sand-hollows to die as Bering died,
'And make a place for Reuben Paine that knows the fight was fair,
'And leave the two that did the wrong to talk it over there!'

Half-steam ahead by guess and lead, for the sun is mostly veiled –
Through fog to fog, by luck and log, sail you as Bering sailed;
And if the light shall lift aright to give your landfall plain,
North and by west, from Zapne Crest you raise the Crosses twain.
Fair marks are they to the inner bay, the reckless poacher knows,
What time the scarred see-catchie[1] *lead their sleek seraglios.*
Ever they hear the floe-pack clear, and the blast of the old bull-whale,

[1] The male seal.

And the deep seal-roar that beats off-shore above the loudest gale.
Ever they wait the winter's hate as the thundering boorga[1] *calls,*
Where northward look they to St George, and westward to St Paul's.
Ever they greet the hunted fleet – lone keels off headlands drear –
When the sealing-schooners flit that way at hazard year by year.
Ever in Yokohama port men tell the tale anew
Of a hidden sea and a hidden fight,
When the Baltic *ran from the* Northern Light,
And the Stralsund *fought the two.*

[1] Hurricane.

McANDREW'S HYMN
1893

Lord, Thou hast made this world below the shadow of a dream,
An', taught by time, I tak' it so – exceptin' always Steam.
From coupler-flange to spindle-guide I see Thy Hand, O God –
Predestination in the stride o' yon connectin'-rod.
John Calvin might ha' forged the same – enorrmous, certain, slow –
Ay, wrought it in the furnace-flame – *my* 'Institutio'.
I cannot get my sleep to-night; old bones are hard to please;
I'll stand the middle watch up here – alone wi' God an' these
My engines, after ninety days o' race an' rack an' strain
Through all the seas of all Thy world, slam-bangin' home again.
Slam-bang too much – they knock a wee – the crosshead-gibs are
  loose,
But thirty thousand mile o' sea has gied them fair excuse . . .
Fine, clear an' dark – a full-draught breeze, wi' Ushant out o' sight,
An' Ferguson relievin' Hay. Old girl, ye'll walk to-night!
His wife's at Plymouth . . . Seventy – One – Two – Three since he
  began –
Three turns for Mistress Ferguson . . . and who's to blame the man?
There's none at any port for me, by drivin' fast or slow,
Since Elsie Campbell went to Thee, Lord, thirty years ago.
(The year the *Sarah Sands* was burned. Oh, roads we used to tread,
Fra' Maryhill to Pollokshaws – fra' Govan to Parkhead!)
Not but they're ceevil on the Board. Ye'll hear Sir Kenneth say:
'Good morrn, McAndrew! Back again? An' how's your bilge
  to-day?'
Miscallin' technicalities but handin' me my chair
To drink Madeira wi' three Earls – the auld Fleet Engineer
That started as a boiler-whelp – when steam and he were low.

I mind the time we used to serve a broken pipe wi' tow!
Ten pound was all the pressure then – Eh! Eh! – a man wad drive;
An' here, our workin' gauges give one hunder sixty-five!
We're creepin' on wi' each new rig – less weight an' larger power;
There'll be the loco-boiler next an' thirty mile an hour!
Thirty an' more. What I ha' seen since ocean-steam began
Leaves me na doot for the machine: but what about the man?
The man that counts, wi' all his runs, one million mile o' sea:
Four time the span from earth to moon . . . How far, O Lord, from
  Thee
That wast beside him night an' day? Ye mind my first typhoon?
It scoughed the skipper on his way to jock wi' the saloon.
Three feet were on the stokehold-floor – just slappin' to an' fro –
An' cast me on a furnace-door. I have the marks to show.
Marks! I ha' marks o' more than burns – deep in my soul an' black,
An' times like this, when things go smooth, my wickudness comes
  back.
The sins o' four an' forty years, all up an' down the seas,
Clack an' repeat like valves half-fed . . . Forgie's our trespasses!
Nights when I'd come on deck to mark, wi' envy in my gaze,
The couples kittlin' in the dark between the funnel-stays;
Years when I raked the Ports wi' pride to fill my cup o' wrong –
Judge not, O Lord, my steps aside at Gay Street in Hong-Kong!
Blot out the wastrel hours of mine in sin when I abode –
Jane Harrigan's an' Number Nine, The Reddick an' Grant Road!
An' waur than all – my crownin' sin – rank blasphemy an' wild.
I was not four and twenty then – Ye wadna judge a child?
I'd seen the Tropics first that run – new fruit, new smells, new air –
How could I tell – blind-fou wi' sun – the Deil was lurkin' there?
By day like playhouse-scenes the shore slid past our sleepy eyes;
By night those soft, lasceevious stars leered from those velvet skies,
In port (we used no cargo-steam) I'd daunder down the streets –
An ijjit grinnin' in a dream – for shells an' parrakeets,

An' walkin'-sticks o' carved bamboo an' blowfish stuffed an' dried –
Fillin' my bunk wi' rubbishry the Chief put overside.
Till, off Sambawa Head, Ye mind, I heard a land-breeze ca',
Milk-warm wi' breath o' spice an' bloom: 'McAndrew, come awa'!'
Firm, clear an' low – no haste, no hate – the ghostly whisper went,
Just statin' eevidential facts beyon' all argument:
'Your mither's God's a graspin' deil, the shadow o' yoursel',
'Got out o' books by meenisters clean daft on Heaven an' Hell.
'They mak' him in the Broomielaw, o' Glasgie cold an' dirt,
'A jealous, pridefu' fetich, lad, that's only strong to hurt.
'Ye'll not go back to Him again an' kiss His red-hot rod,
'But come wi' Us' (Now, who were *They*?) 'an' know the Leevin'
  God,
'That does not kipper souls for sport or break a life in jest,
'But swells the ripenin' cocoanuts an' ripes the woman's breast.'
An' there it stopped – cut off – no more – that quiet, certain voice –
For me, six months o' twenty-four, to leave or take at choice.
'Twas on me like a thunderclap – it racked me through an' through –
Temptation past the show o' speech, unnameable an' new –
The Sin against the Holy Ghost? . . . An' under all, our screw.

That storm blew by but left behind her anchor-shiftin' swell.
Thou knowest all my heart an' mind, Thou knowest, Lord, I fell –
Third on the *Mary Gloster* then, and first that night in Hell!
Yet was Thy Hand beneath my head, about my feet Thy Care –
Fra' Deli clear to Torres Strait, the trial o' despair,
But when we touched the Barrier Reef Thy answer to my prayer! . . .
We dared na run that sea by night but lay an' held our fire,
An' I was drowsin' on the hatch – sick – sick wi' doubt an' tire:
'*Better the sight of eyes that see than wanderin' o' desire!*'
Ye mind that word? Clear as our gongs – again, an' once again,
When rippin' down through coral-trash ran out our moorin'-chain:
An', by Thy Grace, I had the Light to see my duty plain.

Light on the engine-room – no more – bright as our carbons burn.
I've lost it since a thousand times, but never past return!

. . . .

Obsairve! Per annum we'll have here two thousand souls aboard –
Think not I dare to justify myself before the Lord,
But – average fifteen hunder souls safe-borne fra' port to port –
I *am* o' service to my kind. Ye wadna blame the thought?
Maybe they steam from Grace to Wrath – to sin by folly led –
It isna mine to judge their path – their lives are on my head.
Mine at the last – when all is done it all comes back to me,
The fault that leaves six thousand ton a log upon the sea.
We'll tak' one stretch – three weeks an' odd by ony road ye steer –
Fra' Cape Town east to Wellington – ye need an engineer.
Fail there – ye've time to weld your shaft – ay, eat it, ere ye're spoke;
Or make Kerguelen under sail – three jiggers burned wi' smoke!
An' home again – the Rio run: it's no child's play to go
Steamin' to bell for fourteen days o' snow an' floe an' blow.
The bergs like kelpies overside that girn an' turn an' shift
Whaur, grindin' like the Mills o' God, goes by the big South drift.
(Hail, Snow and Ice that praise the Lord. I've met them at their
work,
An' wished we had anither route or they anither kirk.)
Yon's strain, hard strain, o' head an' hand, for though Thy Power
brings
All skill to naught, Ye'll understand a man must think o' things.
Then, at the last, we'll get to port an' hoist their baggage clear –
The passengers, wi' gloves an' canes – an' this is what I'll hear:
'Well, thank ye for a pleasant voyage. The tender's comin' now.'
While I go testin' follower-bolts an' watch the skipper bow.
They've words for every one but me – shake hands wi' half the crew,
Except the dour Scots engineer, the man they never knew.
An' yet I like the wark for all we've dam'-few pickin's here –
No pension, an' the most we'll earn's four hunder pound a year.

Better myself abroad? Maybe. *I'd* sooner starve than sail
Wi' such as call a snifter-rod *ross* . . . French for nightingale.
Commeesion on my stores? Some do; but I cannot afford
To lie like stewards wi' patty-pans. I'm older than the Board.
A bonus on the coal I save? Ou ay, the Scots are close,
But when I grudge the strength Ye gave I'll grudge their food to *those*.
(There's bricks that I might recommend – an' clink the firebars cruel.
No! Welsh – Wangarti at the worst – an' damn all patent fuel!)
Inventions? Ye must stay in port to mak' a patent pay.
My Deeferential Valve-Gear taught me how that business lay.
I blame no chaps wi' clearer heads for aught they make or sell.
I found that I could not invent an' look to these as well.
So, wrestled wi' Apollyon – Nah! – fretted like a bairn –
But burned the workin'-plans last run, wi' all I hoped to earn.
Ye know how hard an Idol dies, an' what that meant to me –
E'en tak' it for a sacrifice acceptable to Thee . . .
Below there! Oiler! What's your wark? Ye find it runnin' hard?
Ye needn't swill the cup wi' oil – this isn't the Cunard!
Ye thought? Ye are not paid to think. Go, sweat that off again!
Tck! Tck! It's deeficult to sweer nor tak' The Name in vain!
Men, ay, an' women, call me stern. Wi' these to oversee,
Ye'll note I've little time to burn on social repartee.
The bairns see what their elders miss; they'll hunt me to an' fro,
Till for the sake of – well, a kiss – I tak' 'em down below.
That minds me of our Viscount loon – Sir Kenneth's kin – the chap
Wi' Russia-leather tennis-shoon an' spar-decked yachtin'-cap.
I showed him round last week, o'er all – an' at the last says he:
'Mister McAndrew, don't you think steam spoils romance at sea?'
Damned ijjit! I'd been doon that morn to see what ailed the throws,
Manholin', on my back – the cranks three inches off my nose.
Romance! Those first-class passengers they like it very well,

Printed an' bound in little books; but why don't poets tell?
I'm sick of all their quirks an' turns – the loves an' doves they dream –
Lord, send a man like Robbie Burns to sing the Song o' Steam!
To match wi' Scotia's noblest speech yon orchestra sublime
Whaurto – uplifted like the Just – the tail-rods mark the time.
The crank-throws give the double-bass, the feed-pump sobs an' heaves,
An' now the main eccentrics start their quarrel on the sheaves:
Her time, her own appointed time, the rocking link-head bides,
Till – hear that note? – the rod's return whings glimmerin' through the guides.
They're all awa'! True beat, full power, the clangin' chorus goes
Clear to the tunnel where they sit, my purrin' dynamoes.
Interdependence absolute, foreseen, ordained, decreed,
To work, Ye'll note, at ony tilt an' every rate o' speed.
Fra' skylight-lift to furnace-bars, backed, bolted, braced an' stayed,
An' singin' like the Mornin' Stars for joy that they are made;
While, out o' touch o' vanity, the sweatin' thrust-block says:
'Not unto us the praise, or man – not unto us the praise!'
Now a' together, hear them lift their lesson – theirs an' mine:
'Law, Orrder, Duty an' Restraint, Obedience, Discipline!'
Mill, forge an' try-pit taught them that when roarin' they arose,
An' whiles I wonder if a soul was gied them wi' the blows.
Oh for a man to weld it then, in one trip-hammer strain,
Till even first-class passengers could tell the meanin' plain!
But no one cares except mysel' that serve an' understand
My seven thousand horse-power here. Eh, Lord! They're grand – they're grand!
Uplift am I? When first in store the new-made beasties stood,
Were Ye cast down that breathed the Word declarin' all things good?
Not so! O' that warld-liftin' joy no after-fall could vex,

Ye've left a glimmer still to cheer the Man – the Arrtifex!
That holds, in spite o' knock and scale, o' friction, waste an' slip,
An' by that light – now, mark my word – we'll build the Perfect
  Ship.
I'll never last to judge her lines or take her curve – not I.
But I ha' lived an' I ha' worked. Be thanks to Thee, Most High!
An' I ha' done what I ha' done – judge Thou if ill or well –
Always Thy Grace preventin' me . . .
    Losh! Yon's the 'Stand-by' bell.
Pilot so soon? His flare it is. The mornin'-watch is set.
Well, God be thanked, as I was sayin', I'm no Pelagian yet.
Now I'll tak' on . . .
  'Morrn, Ferguson. Man, have ye ever thought
What your good leddy costs in coal? . . . I'll burn 'em down to port.

THE SECOND VOYAGE
1903

We've sent our little Cupids all ashore –
  They were frightened, they were tired, they were cold.
Our sails of silk and purple go to store,
  And we've cut away our mast of beaten gold.
      (Foul weather!)
Oh, 'tis hemp and singing pine for to stand against the brine,
  But Love he is our master as of old!

The sea has shorn our galleries away,
  The salt has soiled our gilding past remede;
Our paint is flaked and blistered by the spray,
  Our sides are half a fathom furred in weed.
      (Foul weather!)
And the Doves of Venus fled and the petrels came instead,
  But Love he was our master at our need!

'Was Youth would keep no vigil at the bow,
  'Was Pleasure at the helm too drunk to steer –
We've shipped three able quartermasters now.
  Men call them Custom, Reverence, and Fear.
      (Foul weather!)
They are old and scarred and plain, but we'll run no risk again
  From any Port o' Paphos mutineer!

We seek no more the tempest for delight,
  We skirt no more the indraught and the shoal –
We ask no more of any day or night
  Than to come with least adventure to our goal.
      (Foul weather!)

What we find we needs must brook, but we do not go to look
  Nor tempt the Lord our God that saved us whole.

Yet, caring so, not overmuch we care
  To brace and trim for every foolish blast,
If the squall be pleased to sweep us unaware,
  He may bellow off to leeward like the last.
      (Foul weather!)
We will blame it on the deep (for the watch must have their
    sleep),
  And Love can come and wake us when 'tis past.

Oh, launch them down with music from the beach,
  Oh, warp them out with garlands from the quays –
Most resolute – a damsel unto each –
  New prows that seek the old Hesperides!
      (Foul weather!)
Though we know their voyage is vain, yet we see our path again
  In the saffroned bridesails scenting all the seas!
      (Foul weather!)

THE FIRST CHANTEY
1896

Mine was the woman to me, darkling I found her:
Haling her dumb from the camp, held her and bound her.
Hot rose her tribe on our track ere I had proved her;
Hearing her laugh in the gloom, greatly I loved her.

Swift through the forest we ran, none stood to guard us,
Few were my people and far; then the flood barred us –
Him we call Son of the Sea, sullen and swollen.
Panting we waited the death, stealer and stolen.

Yet ere they came to my lance laid for the slaughter,
Lightly she leaped to a log lapped in the water;
Holding on high and apart skins that arrayed her,
Called she the God of the Wind that He should aid her.

Life had the tree at that word (Praise we the Giver!),
Otter-like left he the bank for the full river,
Far fell their axes behind, flashing and ringing,
Wonder was on me and fear – yet she was singing!

Low lay the land we had left. Now the blue bound us,
Even the Floor of the Gods level around us.
Whisper there was not, nor word, shadow nor showing,
Till the light stirred on the deep, glowing and growing.

Then did He leap to His place flaring from under,
He the Compeller, the Sun, bared to our wonder.
Nay, not a league from our eyes blinded with gazing,
Cleared He the Gate of the World, huge and amazing!

This we beheld (and we live) – the Pit of the Burning!
Then the God spoke to the tree for our returning;
Back to the beach of our flight, fearless and slowly,
Back to our slayers went he; but we were holy.

Men that were hot in that hunt, women that followed,
Babes that were promised our bones, trembled and wallowed
Over the necks of the Tribe crouching and fawning –
Prophet and priestess we came back from the dawning!

THE EXILES' LINE
1890

Now the New Year reviving old desires,
The restless soul to open sea aspires,
  Where the Blue Peter flickers from the fore,
And the grimed stoker feeds the engine-fires.

Coupons, alas, depart with all their rows,
And last year's sea-met loves where Grindlay knows;
  But still the wild wind wakes off Gardafui,
And hearts turn eastward with the P. & O.'s.

Twelve knots an hour, be they more or less –
Oh, slothful mother of much idleness,
  Whom neither rivals spur nor contracts speed!
Nay, bear us gently! Wherefore need we press?

The Tragedy of all our East is laid
On those white decks beneath the awning shade –
  Birth, absence, longing, laughter, love and tears,
And death unmaking ere the land is made.

And midnight madnesses of souls distraught
Whom the cool seas call through the open port,
  So that the table lacks one place next morn,
And for one forenoon men forgo their sport.

The shadow of the rigging to and fro
Sways, shifts, and flickers on the spar-deck's snow,
  And like a giant trampling in his chains,
The screw-blades gasp and thunder deep below;

And, leagued to watch one flying-fish's wings,
Heaven stoops to sea, and sea to Heaven clings;
While, bent upon the ending of his toil,
The hot sun strides, regarding not these things:

For the same wave that meets our stem in spray
Bore Smith of Asia eastward yesterday,
And Delhi Jones and Brown of Midnapore
To-morrow follow on the self-same way.

Linked in the chain of Empire one by one,
Flushed with long leave, or tanned with many a sun,
The Exiles' Line brings out the exiles' line,
And ships them homeward when their work is done.

Yea, heedless of the shuttle through the loom,
The flying keels fulfil the web of doom.
Sorrow or shouting – what is that to them?
Make out the cheque that pays for cabin-room!

And how so many score of times ye flit
With wife and babe and caravan of kit,
Not all thy travels past shall lower one fare,
Not all thy tears abate one pound of it.

And how so high thine earth-born dignity,
Honour and state, go sink it in the sea,
Till that great one upon the quarter-deck,
Brow-bound with gold, shall give thee leave to be.

Indeed, indeed from that same line we swear
Off for all time, and mean it when we swear;
And then, and then we meet the Quartered Flag
And, surely for the last time, pay the fare.

And Green of Kensington, estrayed to view
In three short months the world he never knew,
  Stares with blind eyes upon the Quartered Flag
And sees no more than yellow, red and blue.

But we, the gipsies of the East, but we –
Waifs of the land and wastrels of the sea –
  Come nearer home beneath the Quartered Flag
Than ever home shall come to such as we.

The camp is struck, the bungalow decays,
Dead friends and houses desert mark our ways,
  Till sickness send us down to Prince's Dock
To meet the changeless use of many days.

Bound in the wheel of Empire, one by one,
The chain-gangs of the East from sire to son,
  The Exiles' Line takes out the exiles' line
And ships them homeward when their work is done.

How runs the old indictment? 'Dear and slow,'
So much and twice so much. We gird, but go.
  For all the soul of our sad East is there,
Beneath the house-flag of the P. & O.

THE LONG TRAIL

There's a whisper down the field where the year has shot her yield,
And the ricks stand grey to the sun,
Singing: 'Over then, come over, for the bee has quit the clover,
'And your English summer's done.'

You have heard the beat of the off-shore wind,
And the thresh of the deep-sea rain;
You have heard the song – how long? how long?
Pull out on the trail again!
Ha' done with the Tents of Shem, dear lass,
We've seen the seasons through,
And it's time to turn on the old trail, our own trail, the out trail,
Pull out, pull out, on the Long Trail – the trail that is always new!

It's North you may run to the rime-ringed sun
Or South to the blind Horn's hate;
Or East all the way into Mississippi Bay,
Or West to the Golden Gate –
Where the blindest bluffs hold good, dear lass,
And the wildest tales are true,
And the men bulk big on the old trail, our own trail, the out trail,
And life runs large on the Long Trail – the trail that is always new.

The days are sick and cold, and the skies are grey and old,
And the twice-breathed airs blow damp;
And I'd sell my tired soul for the bucking beam-sea roll
Of a black Bilbao tramp,
With her load-line over her hatch, dear lass,

And a drunken Dago crew,
And her nose held down on the old trail, our own trail, the out trail
From Cadiz south on the Long Trail – the trail that is always new.

There be triple ways to take, of the eagle or the snake,
Or the way of a man with a maid;
But the sweetest way to me is a ship's upon the sea
In the heel of the North-East Trade.
Can you hear the crash on her bows, dear lass,
And the drum of the racing screw,
As she ships it green on the old trail, our own trail, the out trail,
As she lifts and 'scends on the Long Trail – the trail that is always new?

See the shaking funnels roar, with the Peter at the fore,
And the fenders grind and heave,
And the derricks clack and grate, as the tackle hooks the crate,
And the fall-rope whines through the sheave;
It's 'Gang-plank up and in,' dear lass,
It's 'Hawsers warp her through!'
And it's 'All clear aft' on the old trail, our own trail, the out trail,
We're backing down on the Long Trail – the trail that is always new.

O the mutter overside, when the port-fog holds us tied,
And the sirens hoot their dread,
When foot by foot we creep o'er the hueless, viewless deep
To the sob of the questing lead!
It's down by the Lower Hope, dear lass,
With the Gunfleet Sands in view,

Till the Mouse swings green on the old trail, our own trail, the
out trail,
And the Gull Light lifts on the Long Trail – the trail that is
always new.

O the blazing tropic night, when the wake's a welt of light
That holds the hot sky tame,
And the steady fore-foot snores through the planet-powdered floors
Where the scared whale flukes in flame!
Her plates are flaked by the sun, dear lass,
And her ropes are taut with the dew,
For we're booming down on the old trail, our own trail, the out
trail,
We're sagging south on the Long Trail – the trail that is
always new.

Then home, get her home, where the drunken rollers comb,
And the shouting seas drive by,
And the engines stamp and ring, and the wet bows reel and swing,
And the Southern Cross rides high!
Yes, the old lost stars wheel back, dear lass,
That blaze in the velvet blue.
They're all old friends on the old trail, our own trail, the out
trail,
They're God's own guides on the Long Trail – the trail that is
always new.

Fly forward, O my heart, from the Foreland to the Start –
We're steaming all too slow,
And it's twenty thousand mile to our little lazy isle
Where the trumpet-orchids blow!
You have heard the call of the off-shore wind

And the voice of the deep-sea rain;
You have heard the song – how long? – how long?
Pull out on the trail again!

The Lord knows what we may find, dear lass,
And The Deuce knows what we may do –
But we're back once more on the old trail, our own trail, the out trail,
We're down, hull-down, on the Long Trail – the trail that is always new!

A SONG OF THE ENGLISH
1893

Fair is our lot – O goodly is our heritage!
(Humble ye, my people, and be fearful in your mirth!)
For the Lord our God Most High
He hath made the deep as dry,
He hath smote for us a pathway to the ends of all the Earth!

Yea, though we sinned, and our rulers went from righteousness –
Deep in all dishonour though we stained our garments' hem,
Oh, be ye not dismayed,
Though we stumbled and we strayed,
We were led by evil counsellors – the Lord shall deal with them!

Hold ye the Faith – the Faith our Fathers sealèd us;
Whoring not with visions – overwise and overstale.
Except ye pay the Lord
Single heart and single sword,
Of your children in their bondage He shall ask them treble-tale!

Keep ye the Law – be swift in all obedience –
Clear the land of evil, drive the road and bridge the ford.
Make ye sure to each his own
That he reap where he hath sown;
By the peace among Our peoples let men know we serve the Lord!

. . . .

Hear now a song – a song of broken interludes –
A song of little cunning; of a singer nothing worth.
Through the naked words and mean
May ye see the truth between,
As the singer knew and touched it in the ends of all the Earth!

THE COASTWISE LIGHTS

Our brows are bound with spindrift and the weed is on our knees;
Our loins are battered 'neath us by the swinging, smoking seas.
From reef and rock and skerry – over headland, ness, and voe –
The Coastwise Lights of England watch the ships of England go!

Through the endless summer evenings, on the lineless, level floors;
Through the yelling Channel tempest when the siren hoots and
roars –
By day the dipping house-flag and by night the rocket's trail –
As the sheep that graze behind us so we know them where they hail.

We bridge across the dark, and bid the helmsman have a care,
The flash that, wheeling inland, wakes his sleeping wife to prayer.
From our vexed eyries, head to gale, we bind in burning chains
The lover from the sea-rim drawn – his love in English lanes.

We greet the clippers wing-and-wing that race the Southern wool;
We warn the crawling cargo-tanks of Bremen, Leith, and Hull;
To each and all our equal lamp at peril of the sea –
The white wall-sided warships or the whalers of Dundee!

Come up, come in from Eastward, from the guardports of the Morn!
Beat up, beat in from Southerly, O gipsies of the Horn!
Swift shuttles of an Empire's loom that weave us main to main,
The Coastwise Lights of England give you welcome back again!

Go, get you gone up-Channel with the sea-crust on your plates;
Go, get you into London with the burden of your freights!
Haste, for they talk of Empire there, and say, if any seek,
The Lights of England sent you and by silence shall ye speak!

THE SONG OF THE DEAD

Hear now the Song of the Dead – in the North by the torn berg-edges –
They that look still to the Pole, asleep by their hide-stripped sledges.
Song of the Dead in the South – in the sun by their skeleton horses,
Where the warrigal whimpers and bays through the dust of the sere river-courses.

Song of the Dead in the East – in the heat-rotted jungle-hollows,
Where the dog-ape barks in the kloof – in the brake of the buffalo-wallows.
Song of the Dead in the West – in the Barrens, the pass that betrayed them,
Where the wolverine tumbles their packs from the camp and the grave-mound they made them;
Hear now the Song of the Dead!

I

We were dreamers, dreaming greatly, in the man-stifled town;
We yearned beyond the sky-line where the strange roads go down.
Came the Whisper, came the Vision, came the Power with the Need,
Till the Soul that is not man's soul was lent us to lead.
As the deer breaks – as the steer breaks – from the herd where they graze,
In the faith of little children we went on our ways.
Then the wood failed – then the food failed – then the last water dried –
In the faith of little children we lay down and died.
On the sand-drift – on the veldt-side – in the fern-scrub we lay,
That our sons might follow after by the bones on the way.
Follow after – follow after! We have watered the root,

And the bud has come to blossom that ripens for fruit!
Follow after – we are waiting, by the trails that we lost,
For the sounds of many footsteps, for the tread of a host.
Follow after – follow after – for the harvest is sown:
By the bones about the wayside ye shall come to your own!

When Drake went down to the Horn
And England was crowned thereby,
'Twixt seas unsailed and shores unhailed
Our Lodge – our Lodge was born –
(*And England was crowned thereby!*)

Which never shall close again
By day nor yet by night,
While man shall take his life to stake
At risk of shoal or main
(*By day nor yet by night*)

But standeth even so
As now we witness here,
While men depart, of joyful heart,
Adventure for to know
(*As now bear witness here!*)

II

We have fed our sea for a thousand years
And she calls us, still unfed,
Though there's never a wave of all her waves
But marks our English dead:
We have strawed our best to the weed's unrest,
To the shark and the sheering gull.
If blood be the price of admiralty,
Lord God, we ha' paid in full!

There's never a flood goes shoreward now
  But lifts a keel we manned;
There's never an ebb goes seaward now
  But drops our dead on the sand –
But slinks our dead on the sands forlore,
  From the Ducies to the Swin.
If blood be the price of admiralty,
If blood be the price of admiralty,
  Lord God, we ha' paid it in!

We must feed our sea for a thousand years,
  For that is our doom and pride,
As it was when they sailed with the *Golden Hind*,
  Or the wreck that struck last tide –
Or the wreck that lies on the spouting reef
  Where the ghastly blue-lights flare.
If blood be the price of admiralty,
If blood be the price of admiralty,
If blood be the price of admiralty,
  Lord God, we ha' bought it fair!

THE DEEP-SEA CABLES

The wrecks dissolve above us; their dust drops down from afar –
Down to the dark, to the utter dark, where the blind white sea-snakes
  are.
There is no sound, no echo of sound, in the deserts of the deep,
Or the great grey level plains of ooze where the shell-burred cables
  creep.

Here in the womb of the world – here on the tie-ribs of earth
  Words, and the words of men, flicker and flutter and beat –
Warning, sorrow, and gain, salutation and mirth –
  For a Power troubles the Still that has neither voice nor feet.

They have wakened the timeless Things; they have killed their father
Time;
Joining hands in the gloom, a league from the last of the sun.
Hush! Men talk to-day o'er the waste of the ultimate slime,
And a new Word runs between: whispering, 'Let us be one!'

THE SONG OF THE SONS

One from the ends of the earth – gifts at an open door –
Treason has much, but we, Mother, thy sons have more!
From the whine of a dying man, from the snarl of a wolf-pack freed,
Turn, and the world is thine. Mother, be proud of thy seed!
Count, are we feeble or few? Hear, is our speech so rude?
Look, are we poor in the land? Judge, are we men of The Blood?

Those that have stayed at thy knees, Mother, go call them in –
We that were bred overseas wait and would speak with our kin.
Not in the dark do we fight – haggle and flout and gibe;
Selling our love for a price, loaning our hearts for a bribe.
Gifts have we only to-day – Love without promise or fee –
Hear, for thy children speak, from the uttermost parts of the sea!

THE SONG OF THE CITIES

Bombay

Royal and Dower-royal, I the Queen
Fronting thy richest sea with richer hands –
A thousand mills roar through me where I glean
All races from all lands.

Calcutta

Me the Sea-captain loved, the River built,
Wealth sought and Kings adventured life to hold.
Hail England! I am Asia – Power on silt,
Death in my hands, but Gold!

Madras

Clive kissed me on the mouth and eyes and brow,
Wonderful kisses, so that I became
Crowned above Queens – a withered beldame now,
Brooding on ancient fame.

Rangoon

Hail, Mother! Do they call me rich in trade?
Little care I, but hear the shorn priest drone,
And watch my silk-clad lovers, man by maid,
Laugh 'neath my Shwe Dagon.

Singapore

Hail, Mother! East and West must seek my aid
Ere the spent hull may dare the ports afar.
The second doorway of the wide world's trade
Is mine to loose or bar.

Hong-Kong

Hail, Mother! Hold me fast; my Praya sleeps
Under innumerable keels to-day.
Yet guard (and landward), or to-morrow sweeps
Thy warships down the bay!

Halifax

Into the mist my guardian prows put forth,
Behind the mist my virgin ramparts lie,
The Warden of the Honour of the North,
Sleepless and veiled am I!

Quebec and Montreal

Peace is our portion. Yet a whisper rose,
Foolish and causeless, half in jest, half hate.
Now wake we and remember mighty blows,
And, fearing no man, wait!

Victoria

From East to West the circling word has passed,
Till West is East beside our land-locked blue;
From East to West the tested chain holds fast,
The well-forged link rings true!

Capetown

Hail! Snatched and bartered oft from hand to hand,
I dream my dream, by rock and heath and pine,
Of Empire to the northward. Ay, one land
From Lion's Head to Line!

Melbourne

Greeting! Nor fear nor favour won us place,
Got between greed of gold and dread of drouth,
Loud-voiced and reckless as the wild tide-race
That whips our harbour-mouth!

Sydney

Greeting! My birth-stain have I turned to good;
Forcing strong wills perverse to steadfastness:
The first flush of the tropics in my blood,
And at my feet Success!

Brisbane

The northern stock beneath the southern skies –
I build a Nation for an Empire's need,
Suffer a little, and my land shall rise,
Queen over lands indeed!

Hobart

Man's love first found me; man's hate made me Hell;
For my babes' sake I cleansed those infamies.
Earnest for leave to live and labour well,
God flung me peace and ease.

Auckland

Last, loneliest, loveliest, exquisite, apart –
On us, on us the unswerving season smiles,
Who wonder 'mid our fern why men depart
To seek the Happy Isles!

ENGLAND'S ANSWER

Truly ye come of The Blood; slower to bless than to ban,
Little used to lie down at the bidding of any man –
Flesh of the flesh that I bred, bone of the bone that I bare;
Stark as your sons shall be – stern as your fathers were.
Deeper than speech our love, stronger than life our tether,
But we do not fall on the neck nor kiss when we come together.
My arm is nothing weak, my strength is not gone by;
Sons, I have borne many sons, but my dugs are not dry.
Look, I have made ye a place and opened wide the doors,
That ye may talk together, your Barons and Councillors –
Wards of the Outer March, Lords of the Lower Seas,
Ay, talk to your grey mother that bore you on her knees! –
That ye may talk together, brother to brother's face –
Thus for the good of your peoples – thus for the Pride of the Race.
Also, we will make promise. So long as The Blood endures,
I shall know that your good is mine: ye shall feel that my strength is yours:
In the day of Armageddon, at the last great fight of all,
That Our House stand together and the pillars do not fall.
Draw now the threefold knot firm on the ninefold bands,
And the Law that ye make shall be law after the rule of your lands.
This for the waxen Heath, and that for the Wattle-bloom,
This for the Maple-leaf, and that for the Southern Broom.
The Law that ye make shall be law and I do not press my will,
Because ye are Sons of The Blood and call me Mother still.

Now must ye speak to your kinsmen and they must speak to you,
After the use of the English, in straight-flung words and few.
Go to your work and be strong, halting not in your ways,
Baulking the end half-won for an instant dole of praise.
Stand to your work and be wise – certain of sword and pen,
Who are neither children nor Gods, but men in a world of men!

OUR LADY OF THE SNOWS

(Canadian Preferential Tariff, 1897)

A Nation spoke to a Nation,
  A Queen sent word to a Throne:
'Daughter am I in my mother's house,
But mistress in my own.
The gates are mine to open,
  As the gates are mine to close,
And I set my house in order,'
  Said our Lady of the Snows.

'Neither with laughter nor weeping,
  Fear or the child's amaze –
Soberly under the White Man's law
  My white men go their ways.
Not for the Gentiles' clamour –
  Insult or threat of blows –
Bow we the knee to Baal,'
  Said our Lady of the Snows.

'My speech is clean and single,
  I talk of common things –
Words of the wharf and the market-place
  And the ware the merchant brings:
Favour to those I favour,
  But a stumbling-block to my foes.
Many there be that hate us,'
  Said our Lady of the Snows.

'I called my chiefs to council
  In the din of a troubled year;

For the sake of a sign ye would not see,
  And a word ye would not hear.
This is our message and answer;
  This is the path we chose:
For we be also a people,'
  Said our Lady of the Snows.

'Carry the word to my sisters –
  To the Queens of the East and the South.
I have proven faith in the Heritage
  By more than the word of the mouth.
They that are wise may follow
  Ere the world's war-trumpet blows.
But I – I am first in the battle,'
  Said our Lady of the Snows.

A Nation spoke to a Nation,
  A Throne sent word to a Throne:
'Daughter am I in my mother's house,
  But mistress in my own.
The gates are mine to open,
  As the gates are mine to close,
And I abide by my Mother's House,'
Said our Lady of the Snows.

RHODES MEMORIAL, TABLE MOUNTAIN 1905

(From a letter written to Sir Herbert Baker, R.A., when the form of the Memorial was under discussion)

As tho' again – yea, even once again,
  We should rewelcome to our stewardship
The rider with the loose-flung bridle-rein
  And chance-plucked twig for whip,

  The down-turned hat-brim, and the eyes beneath
Alert, devouring – and the imperious hand
Ordaining matters swiftly to bequeath
  Perfect the work he planned.

SUSSEX
1902

God gave all men all earth to love,
  But, since our hearts are small,
Ordained for each one spot should prove
  Belovèd over all;
That, as He watched Creation's birth,
  So we, in godlike mood,
May of our love create our earth
  And see that it is good.

So one shall Baltic pines content,
  As one some Surrey glade,
Or one the palm-grove's droned lament
  Before Levuka's Trade.
Each to his choice, and I rejoice
  The lot has fallen to me
In a fair ground – in a fair ground –
  Yea, Sussex by the sea!

No tender-hearted garden crowns,
  No bosomed woods adorn
Our blunt, bow-headed, whale-backed Downs
  But gnarled and writhen thorn –
Bare slopes where chasing shadows skim,
  And, through the gaps revealed,
Belt upon belt, the wooded, dim,
  Blue goodness of the Weald.

Clean of officious fence or hedge,
  Half-wild and wholly tame,

SUSSEX

The wise turf cloaks the white cliff-edge
  As when the Romans came.
What sign of those that fought and died
  At shift of sword and sword?
The barrow and the camp abide,
  The sunlight and the sward.

Here leaps ashore the full Sou'west
  All heavy-winged with brine,
Here lies above the folded crest
  The Channel's leaden line;
And here the sea-fogs lap and cling,
  And here, each warning each,
The sheep-bells and the ship-bells ring
  Along the hidden beach.

We have no waters to delight
  Our broad and brookless vales –
Only the dewpond on the height
  Unfed, that never fails –
Whereby no tattered herbage tells
  Which way the season flies –
Only our close-bit thyme that smells
  Like dawn in Paradise.

Here through the strong and shadeless days
  The tinkling silence thrills;
Or little, lost, Down churches praise
  The Lord who made the hills:
But here the Old Gods guard their round,
  And, in her secret heart,
The heathen kingdom Wilfrid found
  Dreams, as she dwells, apart.

Though all the rest were all my share,
  With equal soul I'd see
Her nine-and-thirty sisters fair,
  Yet none more fair than she.
Choose ye your need from Thames to Tweed,
  And I will choose instead
Such lands as lie 'twixt Rake and Rye,
  Black Down and Beachy Head.

I will go out against the sun
  Where the rolled scarp retires,
And the Long Man of Wilmington
  Looks naked toward the shires;
And east till doubling Rother crawls
  To find the fickle tide,
By dry and sea-forgotten walls,
  Our ports of stranded pride.

I will go north about the shaws
  And the deep ghylls that breed
Huge oaks and old, the which we hold
  No more than Sussex weed;
Or south where windy Piddinghoe's
  Begilded dolphin veers,
And red beside wide-bankèd Ouse
  Lie down our Sussex steers.

So to the land our hearts we give
  Till the sure magic strike,
And Memory, Use, and Love make live
  Us and our fields alike –
That deeper than our speech and thought,
  Beyond our reason's sway,

Clay of the pit whence we were wrought
  Yearns to its fellow clay.

God gives all men all earth to love,
  But, since man's heart is small,
Ordains for each one spot shall prove
  Belovèd over all.
Each to his choice, and I rejoice
  The lot has fallen to me
In a fair ground – in a fair ground –
  Yea, Sussex by the sea!

THE VAMPIRE[1]
1897

A fool there was and he made his prayer
(Even as you and I!)
To a rag and a bone and a hank of hair
(We called her the woman who did not care)
But the fool he called her his lady fair –
(Even as you and I!)

Oh, the years we waste and the tears we waste
And the work of our head and hand
Belong to the woman who did not know
(*And now we know that she never could know*)
And did not understand!

A fool there was and his goods he spent
(Even as you and I!)
Honour and faith and a sure intent
(And it wasn't the least what the lady meant)
But a fool must follow his natural bent
(Even as you and I!)

Oh, the toil we lost and the spoil we lost
And the excellent things we planned
Belong to the woman who didn't know why
(*And now we know that she never knew why*)
And did not understand!

[1] A set of verses written to accompany a painting by Philip Burne-Jones exhibited in 1897. (Ed.)

THE VAMPIRE

The fool was stripped to his foolish hide
(Even as you and I!)
Which she might have seen when she threw him aside -
(But it isn't on record the lady tried)
So some of him lived but the most of him died –
(Even as you and I!)

And it isn't the shame and it isn't the blame
That stings like a white-hot brand –
It's coming to know that she never knew why
(*Seeing, at last, she could never know why*)
And never could understand!

THE ENGLISH FLAG
1891

Above the portico a flag-staff, bearing the Union Jack, remained fluttering in the flames for some time, but ultimately when it fell the crowds rent the air with shouts, and seemed to see significance in the incident.

Daily Papers.

Winds of the World, give answer! They are whimpering to and fro –
And what should they know of England who only England know? –
The poor little street-bred people that vapour and fume and brag,
They are lifting their heads in the stillness to yelp at the English Flag!

Must we borrow a clout from the Boer – to plaster anew with dirt?
An Irish liar's bandage, or an English coward's shirt?
We may not speak of England; her Flag's to sell or share.
What is the Flag of England? Winds of the World, declare!

The North Wind blew: – 'From Bergen my steel-shod vanguards go;
'I chase your lazy whalers home from the Disko floe.
'By the great North Lights above me I work the will of God,
'And the liner splits on the ice-field or the Dogger fills with cod.

'I barred my gates with iron, I shuttered my doors with flame,
'Because to force my ramparts your nutshell navies came.
I took the sun from their presence, I cut them down with my blast,
And they died, but the Flag of England blew free ere the spirit passed.

The lean white bear hath seen it in the long, long Arctic nights,
The musk-ox knows the standard that flouts the Northern Lights:

'What is the Flag of England? Ye have but my bergs to dare,
'Ye have but my drifts to conquer. Go forth, for it is there!'

The South Wind sighed: – 'From the Virgins my mid-sea course
was ta'en
'Over a thousand islands lost in an idle main,
'Where the sea-egg flames on the coral and the long-backed breakers
croon
'Their endless ocean legends to the lazy, locked lagoon.

'Strayed amid lonely islets, mazed amid outer keys,
'I waked the palms to laughter – I tossed the scud in the breeze.
'Never was isle so little, never was sea so lone,
'But over the scud and the palm-trees an English flag was flown.

'I have wrenched it free from the halliards to hang for a wisp on the
Horn;
'I have chased it north to the Lizard – ribboned and rolled and torn;
'I have spread its folds o'er the dying, adrift in a hopeless sea;
'I have hurled it swift on the slaver, and seen the slave set free.

'My basking sunfish know it, and wheeling albatross,
'Where the lone wave fills with fire beneath the Southern Cross.
'What is the Flag of England? Ye have but my reefs to dare,
'Ye have but my seas to furrow. Go forth, for it is there!'

The East Wind roared: – 'From the Kuriles, the Bitter Seas, I come
'And me men call the Home-Wind, for I bring the English home
'Look – look well to your shipping! By the breath of my mad
typhoon
'I swept your close-packed Praya and beached your best at Kowloon

'The reeling junks behind me and the racing seas before,
'I raped your richest roadstead – I plundered Singapore!

'I set my hand on the Hoogli; as a hooded snake she rose;
'And I flung your stoutest steamers to roost with the startled crows.

'Never the lotos closes, never the wild-fowl wake,
'But a soul goes out on the East Wind that died for England's sake –
'Man or woman or suckling, mother or bride or maid –
'Because on the bones of the English the English Flag is stayed.

'The desert-dust hath dimmed it, the flying wild-ass knows,
'The scared white leopard winds it across the taintless snows.
'What is the Flag of England? Ye have but my sun to dare,
'Ye have but my sands to travel. Go forth, for it is there!'

The West Wind called: – 'In squadrons the thoughtless galleons fly
'That bear the wheat and cattle lest street-bred people die.
'They make my might their porter, they make my house their path,
'Till I loose my neck from their rudder and whelm them all in my wrath.

'I draw the gliding fog-bank as a snake is drawn from the hole.
'They bellow one to the other, the frighted ship-bells toll;
'For day is a drifting terror till I raise the shroud with my breath,
'And they see strange bows above them and the two go locked to death.

'But whether in calm or wrack-wreath, whether by dark or day,
'I heave them whole to the conger or rip their plates away,
'First of the scattered legions, under a shrieking sky,
'Dipping between the rollers, the English Flag goes by.

'The dead dumb fog hath wrapped it – the frozen dews have kissed –
'The naked stars have seen it, a fellow-star in the mist.
'What is the Flag of England? Ye have but my breath to dare,
'Ye have but my waves to conquer. Go forth, for it is there!'

WHEN EARTH'S LAST PICTURE IS PAINTED
1892
(*L'Envoi* to *The Seven Seas*)

When Earth's last picture is painted and the tubes are twisted and
  dried,
When the oldest colours have faded, and the youngest critic has died,
We shall rest, and, faith, we shall need it – lie down for an aeon or
  two,
Till the Master of All Good Workmen shall put us to work anew.

And those that were good shall be happy: they shall sit in a golden
  chair;
They shall splash at a ten-league canvas with brushes of comets' hair.
They shall find real saints to draw from – Magdalene, Peter, and
  Paul;
They shall work for an age at a sitting and never be tired at all!

And only The Master shall praise us, and only The Master shall
  blame;
And no one shall work for money, and no one shall work for fame,
But each for the joy of the working, and each, in his separate star,
Shall draw the Thing as he sees It for the God of Things as They
  are!

THE BALLAD OF EAST AND WEST
1889

Oh, East is East, and West is West, and never the twain shall meet,
Till Earth and Sky stand presently at God's great Judgment Seat;
But there is neither East nor West, Border, nor Breed, nor Birth,
When two strong men stand face to face, though they come from the ends of the earth!

Kamal is out with twenty men to raise the Border-side,
And he has lifted the Colonel's mare that is the Colonel's pride.
He has lifted her out of the stable-door between the dawn and the day,
And turned the calkins upon her feet, and ridden her far away.
Then up and spoke the Colonel's son that led a troop of the Guides:
'Is there never a man of all my men can say where Kamal hides?'
Then up and spoke Mohammed Khan, the son of the Ressaldar:
'If ye know the track of the morning-mist, ye know where his pickets are.
'At dusk he harries the Abazai – at dawn he is into Bonair,
'But he must go by Fort Bukloh to his own place to fare.
'So if ye gallop to Fort Bukloh as fast as a bird can fly,
'By the favour of God ye may cut him off ere he win to the Tongue of Jagai.
'But if he be past the Tongue of Jagai, right swiftly turn ye then,
'For the length and the breadth of that grisly plain is sown with Kamal's men.
'There is rock to the left, and rock to the right, and low lean thorn between,
'And ye may hear a breech-bolt snick where never a man is seen.'
The Colonel's son has taken horse, and a raw rough dun was he,

With the mouth of a bell and the heart of Hell and the head of a gallows-tree.
The Colonel's son to the Fort has won, they bid him stay to eat –
Who rides at the tail of a Border thief, he sits not long at his meat.
He's up and away from Fort Bukloh as fast as he can fly,
Till he was aware of his father's mare in the gut of the Tongue of Jagai,
Till he was aware of his father's mare with Kamal upon her back,
And when he could spy the white of her eye, he made the pistol crack.
He has fired once, he has fired twice, but the whistling ball went wide.
'Ye shoot like a soldier,' Kamal said. 'Show now if ye can ride!'
It's up and over the Tongue of Jagai, as blown dust-devils go,
The dun he fled like a stag of ten, but the mare like a barren doe.
The dun he leaned against the bit and slugged his head above,
But the red mare played with the snaffle-bars, as a maiden plays with a glove.
There was rock to the left and rock to the right, and low lean thorn between,
And thrice he heard a breech-bolt snick tho' never a man was seen.
They have ridden the low moon out of the sky, their hoofs drum up the dawn,
The dun he went like a wounded bull, but the mare like a new-roused fawn.
The dun he fell at a water-course – in a woeful heap fell he,
And Kamal has turned the red mare back, and pulled the rider free.
He has knocked the pistol out of his hand – small room was there to strive,
''Twas only by favour of mine,' quoth he, 'ye rode so long alive:
'There was not a rock for twenty mile, there was not a clump of tree,
'But covered a man of my own men with his rifle cocked on his knee.

'If I had raised my bridle-hand, as I have held it low,
'The little jackals that flee so fast were feasting all in a row.
'If I had bowed my head on my breast, as I have held it high,
'The kite that whistles above us now were gorged till she could not fly.'
Lightly answered the Colonel's son: 'Do good to bird and beast,
'But count who come for the broken meats before thou makest a feast.
'If there should follow a thousand swords to carry my bones away,
'Belike the price of a jackal's meal were more than a thief could pay.
'They will feed their horse on the standing crop, their men on the garnered grain.
'The thatch of the byres will serve their fires when all the cattle are slain.
'But if thou thinkest the price be fair, – thy brethren wait to sup,
'The hound is kin to the jackal-spawn, – howl, dog, and call them up!
'And if thou thinkest the price be high, in steer and gear and stack,
'Give me my father's mare again, and I'll fight my own way back!'
Kamal has gripped him by the hand and set him upon his feet.
'No talk shall be of dogs,' said he, 'when wolf and grey wolf meet.
'May I eat dirt if thou hast hurt of me in deed or breath;
'What dam of lances brought thee forth to jest at the dawn with Death?'
Lightly answered the Colonel's son: 'I hold by the blood of my clan:
'Take up the mare for my father's gift – by God, she has carried a man!'
The red mare ran to the Colonel's son, and nuzzled against his breast;
'We be two strong men,' said Kamal then, 'but she loveth the younger best.
'So she shall go with a lifter's dower, my turquoise-studded rein,
'My 'broidered saddle and saddle-cloth, and silver stirrups twain.'

The Colonel's son a pistol drew, and held it muzzle-end,
'Ye have taken the one from a foe,' said he. 'Will ye take the mate from a friend?'
'A gift for a gift,' said Kamal straight; 'a limb for the risk of a limb.
'Thy father has sent his son to me, I'll send my son to him!'
With that he whistled his only son, that dropped from a mountain-crest –
He trod the ling like a buck in spring, and he looked like a lance in rest.
'Now here is thy master,' Kamal said, 'who leads a troop of the Guides,
'And thou must ride at his left side as shield on shoulder rides.
'Till Death or I cut loose the tie, at camp and board and bed,
'Thy life is his – thy fate it is to guard him with thy head.
'So, thou must eat the White Queen's meat, and all her foes are thine,
'And thou must harry thy father's hold for the peace of the Border-line.
'And thou must make a trooper tough and hack thy way to power –
'Belike they will raise thee to Ressaldar when I am hanged in Peshawur!'

They have looked each other between the eyes, and there they found no fault.
They have taken the Oath of the Brother-in-Blood on leavened bread and salt:
They have taken the Oath of the Brother-in-Blood on fire and fresh-cut sod,
On the hilt and the haft of the Khyber knife, and the Wondrous Names of God.
The Colonel's son he rides the mare and Kamal's boy the dun,
And two have come back to Fort Bukloh where there went forth but one.

And when they drew to the Quarter-Guard, full twenty swords flew clear –
There was not a man but carried his feud with the blood of the mountaineer.
'Ha' done! ha' done!' said the Colonel's son. 'Put up the steel at your sides!
'Last night ye had struck at a Border thief – to-night 'tis a man of the Guides!'

Oh, East is East, and West is West, and never the twain shall meet,
Till Earth and Sky stand presently at God's great Judgment Seat;
But there is neither East nor West, Border, nor Breed, nor Birth,
When two strong men stand face to face, though they come from the ends of the earth!

THE BALLAD OF BOH DA THONE
1888
(Burma War, 1883–85)

This is the ballad of Boh Da Thone,
Erst a Pretender to Theebaw's throne,
Who harried the District of Alalone:
How he met with his fate and the V.P.P.[1]
At the hand of Harendra Mukerji,
Senior Gomashta, G.B.T.[2]

Boh Da Thone was a warrior bold:
His sword and his rifle were bossed with gold.

And the Peacock Banner his henchmen bore
Was stiff with bullion, but stiffer with gore.

He shot at the strong and he slashed at the weak
From the Salween scrub to the Chindwin teak:

He crucified noble, he scarified mean,
He filled old ladies with kerosene:

While over the water the papers cried,
'The patriot fights for his countryside!'

But little they cared for the Native Press,
The worn white soldiers in khaki dress,

Who tramped through the jungle and camped in the byre,
Who died in the swamp and were tombed in the mire,

[1] Value Payable Post = Collect on Delivery.
[2] Head Clerk, Government Bullock Train.

Who gave up their lives, at the Queen's Command,
For the Pride of their Race and the Peace of the Land.

Now, first of the foemen of Boh Da Thone
Was Captain O'Neil of the Black Tyrone,

And his was a Company, seventy strong,
Who hustled that dissolute Chief along.

There were lads from Galway and Louth and Meath
Who went to their death with a joke in their teeth,

And worshipped with fluency, fervour, and zeal
The mud on the boot-heels of 'Crook' O'Neil.

But ever a blight on their labours lay,
And ever their quarry would vanish away,

Till the sun-dried boys of the Black Tyrone
Took a brotherly interest in Boh Da Thone,

And, sooth, if pursuit in possession ends,
The Boh and his trackers were best of friends.

The word of a scout – a march by night –
A rush through the mist – a scattering fight –

A volley from cover – a corpse in the clearing –
A glimpse of a loin-cloth and heavy jade earring –

The flare of a village – the tally of slain –
And . . . the Boh was abroad on the raid again!

They cursed their luck, as the Irish will,
They gave him credit for cunning and skill,

They buried their dead, they bolted their beef,
And started anew on the track of the thief,

Till, in place of the 'Kalends of Greece,' men said,
'When Crook and his darlings come back with the head.'

They had hunted the Boh from the hills to the plain –
He doubled and broke for the hills again:

They had crippled his power for rapine and raid,
They had routed him out of his pet stockade,

And at last, they came, when the Daystar tired,
To a camp deserted – a village fired.

A black cross blistered the morning-gold,
But the body upon it was stark and cold.

The wind of the dawn went merrily past,
The high grass bowed her plumes to the blast,

And out of the grass, on a sudden, broke
A spirtle of fire, a whorl of smoke –

And Captain O'Neil of the Black Tyrone
Was blessed with a slug in the ulnar-bone –
The gift of his enemy Boh Da Thone.

(Now a slug that is hammered from telegraph-wire
Is a thorn in the flesh and a rankling fire.)

. . . . .

The shot-wound festered – as shot-wounds may
In a steaming barrack at Mandalay.

The left arm throbbed, and the Captain swore,
'I'd like to be after the Boh once more!'

The fever held him – the Captain said,
'I'd give a hundred to look at his head!'

The Hospital punkahs creaked and whirred,
But Babu Harendra (Gomashta) heard.

He thought of the cane-brake, green and dank,
That girdled his home by the Dacca tank.

He thought of his wife and his High School son,
He thought – but abandoned the thought – of a gun.

His sleep was broken by visions dread
Of a shining Boh with a silver head.

He kept his counsel and went his way,
And swindled the cartmen of half their pay.

. . . . . .

And the months went on, as the worst must do,
And the Boh returned to the raid anew.

But the Captain had quitted the long-drawn strife,
And in far Simoorie had taken a wife;

And she was a damsel of delicate mould,
With hair like the sunshine and heart of gold,

And little she knew the arms that embraced
Had cloven a man from the brow to the waist:

And little she knew that the loving lips
Had ordered a quivering life's eclipse,

Or the eye that lit at her lightest breath
Had glared unawed in the Gates of Death.

(For these be matters a man would hide,
As a general rule, from an innocent Bride.)

And little the Captain thought of the past,
And, of all men, Babu Harendra last.

. . . . . .

But slow, in the sludge of the Kathun road,
The Government Bullock Train toted its load.

Speckless and spotless and shining with *ghi*,
In the rearmost cart sat the Babu-jee;

And ever a phantom before him fled
Of a scowling Boh with a silver head.

Then the lead-cart stuck, though the coolies slaved,
And the cartmen flogged and the escort raved,

And out of the jungle, with yells and squeals,
Pranced Boh Da Thone, and his gang at his heels!

Then belching blunderbuss answered back
The Snider's snarl and the carbine's crack,

And the blithe revolver began to sing
To the blade that twanged on the locking-ring,

And the brown flesh blued where the bayonet kissed,
As the steel shot back with a wrench and a twist,

And the great white oxen with onyx eyes
Watched the souls of the dead arise,

And over the smoke of the fusillade
The Peacock Banner staggered and swayed.

The Babu shook at the horrible sight,
And girded his ponderous loins for flight,

But Fate had ordained that the Boh should start
On a lone-hand raid of the rearmost cart,

And out of that cart, with a bellow of woe,
The Babu fell – flat on the top of the Boh!

For years had Harendra served the State,
To the growth of his purse and the girth of his *pêt*.[1]

There were twenty stone, as the tally-man knows,
On the broad of the chest of this best of Bohs.

And twenty stone from a height discharged
Are bad for a Boh with a spleen enlarged.

Oh, short was the struggle – severe was the shock –
He dropped like a bullock – he lay like a block;

And the Babu above him, convulsed with fear,
Heard the labouring life-breath hissed out in his ear.

And thus in a fashion undignified
The princely pest of the Chindwin died.

. . . . . .

Turn now to Simoorie, where, all at his ease,
The Captain is petting the Bride on his knees,

[1] Stomach.

Where the *whit* of the bullet, the wounded man's scream
Are mixed as the mist of some devilish dream –

Forgotten, forgotten the sweat of the shambles
Where the hill-daisy blooms and the grey monkey gambols,

From the sword-belt set free and released from the steel,
The Peace of the Lord is on Captain O'Neil!

Up the hill to Simoorie – most patient of drudges –
The bags on his shoulder, the mail-runner trudges.

'For Captain O'Neil Sahib. One hundred and ten
'Rupees to collect on delivery.'
Then

(Their breakfast was stopped while the screw-jack and hammer
Tore waxcloth, split teak-wood, and chipped out the
dammer;[1])
Open-eyed, open-mouthed, on the napery's snow,
With a crash and a thud, rolled – the Head of the Boh!

And gummed to the scalp was a letter which ran:–
'IN FIELDING FORCE SERVICE.
'*Encampment*,
'10th Jan.

'Dear Sir, – I have honour to send, *as you said*,
'For final approval (see under) Boh's Head;

'Was took by myself in most bloody affair.
'By High Education brought pressure to bear.

[1] Native sealing-wax.

'Now violate Liberty, time being bad,
'To mail V.P.P. (rupees hundred) Please add

'Whatever Your Honour can pass. Price of Blood
'Much cheap at one hundred, and children want food.

'So trusting Your Honour will somewhat retain
'True love and affection for Govt. Bullock Train,

'And show awful kindness to satisfy me,
'I am,
'Graceful Master,
'Your
'H. MUKERJI.'

. . . . .

As the rabbit is drawn to the rattlesnake's power,
As the smoker's eye fills at the opium hour,

As a horse reaches up to the manger above,
As the waiting ear yearns for the whisper of love,

From the arms of the Bride, iron-visaged and slow,
The Captain bent down to the Head of the Boh.

And e'en as he looked on the Thing where It lay
'Twixt the winking new spoons and the napkins' array,

The freed mind fled back to the long-ago days –
The hand-to-hand scuffle – the smoke and the blaze –

The forced march at night and the quick rush at dawn –
The banjo at twilight, the burial ere morn –

The stench of the marshes – the raw, piercing smell
When the overhand stabbing-cut silenced the yell –

The oaths of his Irish that surged when they stood
Where the black crosses hung o'er the Kuttamow flood.

As a derelict ship drifts away with the tide
The Captain went out on the Past from his Bride,

Back, back, through the springs to the chill of the year,
When he hunted the Boh from Maloon to Tsaleer.

As the shape of a corpse dimmers up through deep water,
In his eye lit the passionless passion of slaughter,

And men who had fought with O'Neil for the life
Had gazed on his face with less dread than his wife.

For she who had held him so long could not hold him –
Though a four-month Eternity should have controlled him! –

But watched the Twin Terror – the head turned to head –
The scowling, scarred Black, and the flushed savage Red –

The spirit that changed from her knowing and flew to
Some grim hidden Past she had never a clue to.

But It knew as It grinned, for he touched it unfearing,
And muttered aloud, 'So you kept that jade earring!'

Then nodded, and kindly, as friend nods to friend,
'Old man, you fought well, but you lost in the end.'

. . . . . .

The visions departed, and Shame followed Passion: –
'He took what I said in this horrible fashion?

'*I'll* write to Harendra!' With language unsainted
The Captain came back to the Bride . . . who had fainted.

. . . . . .

And this is a fiction? No. Go to Simoorie
And look at their baby, a twelve-month-old Houri,

A pert little, Irish-eyed Kathleen Mavournin –
She's always about on the Mall of a mornin' –

And you'll see, if her right shoulder-strap is displaced,
This: *Gules* upon *argent*, a Boh's Head, *erased!*

THE LESSON
1899–1902
(Boer War)

Let us admit it fairly, as a business people should,
We have had no end of a lesson: it will do us no end of good.

Not on a single issue, or in one direction or twain,
But conclusively, comprehensively, and several times and again,
Were all our most holy illusions knocked higher than Gilderoy's kite.
We have had a jolly good lesson, and it serves us jolly well right!

This was not bestowèd us under the trees, nor yet in the shade of a
tent,
But swingingly, over eleven degrees of a bare brown continent.
From Lamberts to Delagoa Bay, and from Pietersburg to Sutherland,
Fell the phenomenal lesson we learned – with a fulness accorded no
other land.

It was our fault, and our very great fault, and *not* the judgment of
Heaven.
We made an Army in our own image, on an island nine by seven,
Which faithfully mirrored its makers' ideals, equipment, and mental
attitude –
And so we got our lesson: and we ought to accept it with gratitude.

We have spent two hundred million pounds to prove the fact once
more,
That horses are quicker than men afoot, since two and two make
four;

And horses have four legs, and men have two legs, and two into four
goes twice,
And nothing over except our lesson – and very cheap at the price.

For remember (this our children shall know: we are too near for that
knowledge)
Not our mere astonied camps, but Council and Creed and College –
All the obese, unchallenged old things that stifle and overlie us –
Have felt the effects of the lesson we got – an advantage no money
could buy us!

Then let us develop this marvellous asset which we alone command,
And which, it may subsequently transpire, will be worth as much as
the Rand.
Let us approach this pivotal fact in a humble yet hopeful mood –
We have had no end of a lesson. It will do us no end of good!

It was our fault, and our very great fault – and now we must turn it
to use.
We have forty million reasons for failure, but not a single excuse.
So the more we work and the less we talk the better results we shall
get.
We have had an Imperial lesson. It may make us an Empire yet!

THE ISLANDERS
1902

No doubt but ye are the People – your throne is above the King's.
Whoso speaks in your presence must say acceptable things:
Bowing the head in worship, bending the knee in fear –
Bringing the word well smoothen – such as a King should hear.

Fenced by your careful fathers, ringed by your leaden seas,
Long did ye wake in quiet and long lie down at ease;
Till ye said of Strife, 'What is it?' of the Sword, 'It is far from our ken';
Till ye made a sport of your shrunken hosts and a toy of your armèd men.
Ye stopped your ears to the warning – ye would neither look nor heed –
Ye set your leisure before their toil and your lusts above their need.
Because of your witless learning and your beasts of warren and chase,
Ye grudged your sons to their service and your fields for their camping-place.
Ye forced them glean in the highways the straw for the bricks they brought;
Ye forced them follow in byways the craft that ye never taught.
Ye hampered and hindered and crippled; ye thrust out of sight and away
Those that would serve you for honour and those that served you for pay.
Then were the judgments loosened; then was your shame revealed,
At the hands of a little people, few but apt in the field.
Yet ye were saved by a remnant (and your land's long-suffering star)

When your strong men cheered in their millions while your striplings went to the war.
Sons of the sheltered city – unmade, unhandled, unmeet –
Ye pushed them raw to the battle as ye picked them raw from the street.
And what did ye look they should compass? Warcraft learned in a breath,
Knowledge unto occasion at the first far view of Death?
So? And ye train your horses and the dogs ye feed and prize?
How are the beasts more worthy than the souls, your sacrifice?
But ye said, 'Their valour shall show them'; but ye said, 'The end is close.'
And ye sent them comfits and pictures to help them harry your foes:
And ye vaunted your fathomless power, and ye flaunted your iron pride,
Ere – ye fawned on the Younger Nations for the men who could shoot and ride!
Then ye returned to your trinkets; then ye contented your souls
With the flannelled fools at the wicket or the muddied oafs at the goals.
Given to strong delusion, wholly believing a lie,
Ye saw that the land lay fenceless, and ye let the months go by
Waiting some easy wonder, hoping some saving sign –
Idle – openly idle – in the lee of the forespent Line.
Idle – except for your boasting – and what is your boasting worth
If ye grudge a year of service to the lordliest life on earth?
Ancient, effortless, ordered, cycle on cycle set,
Life so long untroubled, that ye who inherit forget
It was not made with the mountains, it is not one with the deep.
Men, not gods, devised it. Men, not gods, must keep.
Men, not children, servants, or kinsfolk called from afar,
But each man born in the Island broke to the matter of war.
Soberly and by custom taken and trained for the same,

Each man born in the Island entered at youth to the game –
As it were almost cricket, not to be mastered in haste,
But after trial and labour, by temperance, living chaste.
As it were almost cricket – as it were even your play,
Weighed and pondered and worshipped, and practised day and day.
So ye shall bide sure-guarded when the restless lightnings wake
In the womb of the blotting war-cloud, and the pallid nations quake.
So, at the haggard trumpets, instant your soul shall leap
Forthright, accoutred, accepting – alert from the wells of sleep.
So at the threat ye shall summon – so at the need ye shall send
Men, not children or servants, tempered and taught to the end;
Cleansed of servile panic, slow to dread or despise,
Humble because of knowledge, mighty by sacrifice . . .
But ye say, 'It will mar our comfort.' Ye say, 'It will minish our trade.'
Do ye wait for the spattered shrapnel ere ye learn how a gun is laid?
For the low, red glare to southward when the raided coast-towns burn?
(Light ye shall have on that lesson, but little time to learn.)
Will ye pitch some white pavilion, and lustily even the odds,
With nets and hoops and mallets, with rackets and bats and rods?
Will the rabbit war with your foemen – the red deer horn them for hire?
Your kept cock-pheasant keep you? – he is master of many a shire.
Arid, aloof, incurious, unthinking, unthanking, gelt,
Will ye loose your schools to flout them till their brow-beat columns melt?
Will ye pray them or preach them, or print them, or ballot them back from your shore?
Will your workmen issue a mandate to bid them strike no more?
Will ye rise and dethrone your rulers? (Because ye were idle both?
Pride by Insolence chastened? Indolence purged by Sloth?)
No doubt but ye are the People; who shall make you afraid?

Also your gods are many; no doubt but your gods shall aid.
Idols of greasy altars built for the body's ease;
Proud little brazen Baals and talking fetishes;
Teraphs of sept and party and wise wood-pavement gods –
These shall come down to the battle and snatch you from under the
  rods?
From the gusty, flickering gun-roll with viewless salvoes rent,
And the pitted hail of the bullets that tell not whence they were sent.
When ye are ringed as with iron, when ye are scourged as with
  whips,
When the meat is yet in your belly, and the boast is yet on your lips;
When ye go forth at morning and the noon beholds you broke,
Ere ye lie down at even, your remnant, under the yoke?

No doubt but ye are the People – absolute, strong, and wise;
Whatever your heart has desired ye have not withheld from your eyes.
On your own heads, in your own hands, the sin and the saving lies!

THE DYKES
1902

We have no heart for the fishing – we have no hand for the oar –
All that our fathers taught us of old pleases us now no more.
All that our own hearts bid us believe we doubt where we do not deny –
There is no proof in the bread we eat nor rest in the toil we ply.

Look you, our foreshore stretches far through sea-gate, dyke, and groin –
Made land all, that our fathers made, where the flats and the fairway join.
They forced the sea a sea-league back. They died, and their work stood fast.
We were born to peace in the lee of the dykes, but the time of our peace is past.

Far off, the full tide clambers and slips, mouthing and testing all,
Nipping the flanks of the water-gates, baying along the wall;
Turning the shingle, returning the shingle, changing the set of the sand . . .
We are too far from the beach, men say, to know how the outworks stand.

So we come down, uneasy, to look; uneasily pacing the beach.
These are the dykes our fathers made: we have never known a breach.
Time and again has the gale blown by and we were not afraid;
Now we come only to look at the dykes – at the dykes our fathers made.

THE DYKES

O'er the marsh where the homesteads cower apart the harried sun-
light flies,
Shifts and considers, wanes and recovers, scatters and sickens and
dies –
An evil ember bedded in ash – a spark blown west by the wind . . .
We are surrendered to night and the sea – the gale and the tide
behind!

At the bridge of the lower saltings the cattle gather and blare,
Roused by the feet of running men, dazed by the lantern-glare.
Unbar and let them away for their lives – the levels drown as they
stand,
Where the flood-wash forces the sluices aback and the ditches
deliver inland.

Ninefold deep to the top of the dykes the galloping breakers stride,
And their overcarried spray is a sea – a sea on the landward side.
Coming, like stallions they paw with their hooves, going they snatch
with their teeth,
Till the bents and the furze and the sand are dragged out, and the
old-time hurdles beneath.

Bid men gather fuel for fire, the tar, the oil, and the tow –
Flame we shall need, not smoke, in the dark if the riddled sea-banks
go.
Bid the ringers watch in the tower (who knows how the dawn shall
prove?)
Each with his rope between his feet and the trembling bells above.

Now we can only wait till the day, wait and apportion our shame.
These are the dykes our fathers left, but we would not look to the
same.

Time and again were we warned of the dykes, time and again we delayed:
Now, it may fall, we have slain our sons, as our fathers we have betrayed.

. . . .

Walking along the wreck of the dykes, watching the work of the seas!
These were the dykes our fathers made to our great profit and ease.
But the peace is gone and the profit is gone, with the old sure days withdrawn . . .
That our own houses show as strange when we come back in the dawn!

'THE CITY OF BRASS'
1909

'Here was a people whom after their works thou shalt see wept over for their lost dominion: and in this palace is the last information respecting lords collected in the dust.'

The Arabian Nights.

In a land that the sand overlays – the ways to her gates are untrod –
A multitude ended their days whose fates were made splendid by God,
Till they grew drunk and were smitten with madness and went to their fall,
And of these is a story written: but Allah Alone knoweth all!

When the wine stirred in their heart their bosoms dilated.
They rose to suppose themselves kings over all things created –
To decree a new earth at a birth without labour or sorrow –
To declare: 'We prepare it to-day and inherit to-morrow.'
They chose themselves prophets and priests of minute understanding,
Men swift to see done, and outrun, their extremest commanding –
Of the tribe which describe with a jibe the perversions of Justice –
Panders avowed to the crowd whatsoever its lust is.

Swiftly these pulled down the walls that their fathers had made them –
The impregnable ramparts of old, they razed and relaid them
As playgrounds of pleasure and leisure, with limitless entries,
And havens of rest for the wastrels where once walked the sentries;
And because there was need of more pay for the shouters and marchers,
They disbanded in face of their foemen their yeomen and archers.

They replied to their well-wishers' fears – to their enemies' laughter,
Saying: 'Peace! We have fashioned a God Which shall save us hereafter.
We ascribe all dominion to man in his factions conferring,
And have given to numbers the Name of the Wisdom unerring.'

They said: 'Who has hate in his soul? Who has envied his neighbour?
Let him arise and control both that man and his labour.'
They said: 'Who is eaten by sloth? Whose unthrift has destroyed him?
He shall levy a tribute from all because none have employed him.'
They said: 'Who hath toiled, who hath striven, and gathered possession?
Let him be spoiled. He hath given full proof of transgression.'
They said: 'Who is irked by the Law? *Though we may not remove it,*
If he lend us his aid in this raid, we will set him above it!'
So the robber did judgment again upon such as displeased him,
The slayer, too, boasted his slain, and the judges released him.

As for their kinsmen far off, on the skirts of the nation,
They harried all earth to make sure none escaped reprobation.
They awakened unrest for a jest in their newly-won borders,
And jeered at the blood of their brethren betrayed by their orders.
They instructed the ruled to rebel, their rulers to aid them;
And, since such as obeyed them not fell, their Viceroys obeyed them.
When the riotous set them at naught they said: 'Praise the upheaval!
For the show and the word and the thought of Dominion is evil!'
They unwound and flung from them with rage, as a rag that defiled them,
The imperial gains of the age which their forefathers piled them.
They ran panting in haste to lay waste and embitter for ever
The Wellsprings of Wisdom and Strength which are Faith and Endeavour.

They nosed out and digged up and dragged forth and exposed to derision
All doctrine of purpose and worth and restraint and prevision:

And it ceased, and God granted them all things for which they had striven,
And the heart of a beast in the place of a man's heart was given . . .

. . . .

When they were fullest of wine and most flagrant in error,
Out of the sea rose a sign – out of Heaven a terror.
Then they saw, then they heard, then they knew – for none troubled to hide it,
An host had prepared their destruction, but still they denied it.
They denied what they dared not abide if it came to the trial;
But the Sword that was forged while they lied did not heed their denial.
It drove home, and no time was allowed to the crowd that was driven.
The preposterous-minded were cowed – they thought time would be given.
There was no need of a steed nor a lance to pursue them;
It was decreed their own deed, and not chance, should undo them.
The tares they had laughingly sown were ripe to the reaping.
The trust they had leagued to disown was removed from their keeping.
The eaters of other men's bread, the exempted from hardship,
The excusers of impotence fled, abdicating their wardship,
For the hate they had taught through the State brought the State no defender,
And it passed from the roll of the Nations in headlong surrender!

THE OLD MEN
1902

This is our lot if we live so long and labour unto the end –
That we outlive the impatient years and the much too patient friend:
And because we know we have breath in our mouth and think we have thoughts in our head,
We shall assume that we are alive, whereas we are really dead.

We shall not acknowledge that old stars fade or stronger planets arise
(That the sere bush buds or the desert blooms or the ancient well-head dries),
Or any new compass wherewith new men adventure 'neath new skies.

We shall lift up the ropes that constrained our youth, to bind on our children's hands;
We shall call to the water below the bridges to return and replenish our lands;
We shall harness horses (Death's own pale horses) and scholarly plough the sands.

We shall lie down in the eye of the sun for lack of a light on our way –
We shall rise up when the day is done and chirrup, 'Behold, it is day!'
We shall abide till the battle is won ere we amble into the fray.

We shall peck out and discuss and dissect, and evert and extrude to our mind,

The flaccid tissues of long-dead issues offensive to God and man-
kind –
(Precisely like vultures over an ox that the Army has left behind).

We shall make walk preposterous ghosts of the glories we once
created –
Immodestly smearing from muddled palettes amazing pigments
mismated –
And our friends will weep when we ask them with boasts if our
natural force be abated.

The Lamp of our Youth will be utterly out, but we shall subsist on
the smell of it;
And whatever we do, we shall fold our hands and suck our gums and
think well of it.
Yes, we shall be perfectly pleased with our work, and that is the
Perfectest Hell of it!

This is our lot if we live so long and listen to those who love us –
*That we are shunned by the people about and shamed by the Powers
above us.*
Wherefore be free of your harness betimes; but, being free, be assured,
*That he who hath not endured to the death, from his birth he hath never
endured!*

THE WHITE MAN'S BURDEN
1899
(The United States and the Philippine Islands)

Take up the White Man's burden –
  Send forth the best ye breed –
Go bind your sons to exile
  To serve your captives' need;
To wait in heavy harness
  On fluttered folk and wild –
Your new-caught, sullen peoples,
  Half devil and half child.

Take up the White Man's Burden –
  In patience to abide,
To veil the threat of terror
  And check the show of pride;
By open speech and simple,
  An hundred times made plain,
To seek another's profit,
  And work another's gain.

Take up the White Man's burden –
  The savage wars of peace –
Fill full the mouth of Famine
  And bid the sickness cease;
And when your goal is nearest
  The end for others sought,
Watch Sloth and heathen Folly
  Bring all your hope to nought.

Take up the White Man's burden –
  No tawdry rule of kings,
But toil of serf and sweeper –
  The tale of common things.
The ports ye shall not enter,
  The roads ye shall not tread,
Go make them with your living,
  And mark them with your dead!

Take up the White Man's burden –
  And reap his old reward:
The blame of those ye better,
  The hate of those ye guard –
The cry of hosts ye humour
  (Ah, slowly!) toward the light: –
'Why brought ye us from bondage,
  'Our loved Egyptian night?'

Take up the White Man's burden –
  Ye dare not stoop to less –
Nor call too loud on Freedom
  To cloak your weariness;
By all ye cry or whisper,
  By all ye leave or do,
The silent, sullen peoples
  Shall weigh your Gods and you.

Take up the White Man's burden –
  Have done with childish days –
The lightly proffered laurel,
  The easy, ungrudged praise.
Comes now, to search your manhood
  Through all the thankless years,
Cold-edged with dear-bought wisdom,
  The judgment of your peers!

RECESSIONAL
1897

God of our fathers, known of old,
  Lord of our far-flung battle-line,
Beneath whose awful Hand we hold
  Dominion over palm and pine –
Lord God of Hosts, be with us yet,
Lest we forget – lest we forget!

The tumult and the shouting dies;
  The Captains and the Kings depart:
Still stands Thine ancient sacrifice,
  An humble and a contrite heart.
Lord God of Hosts, be with us yet,
Lest we forget – lest we forget!

Far-called, our navies melt away;
  On dune and headland sinks the fire:
Lo, all our pomp of yesterday
  Is one with Nineveh and Tyre!
Judge of the Nations, spare us yet,
Lest we forget – lest we forget!

If, drunk with sight of power, we loose
  Wild tongues that have not Thee in awe,
Such boastings as the Gentiles use,
  Or lesser breeds without the Law –
Lord God of Hosts, be with us yet,
Lest we forget – lest we forget!

For heathen heart that puts her trust
   In reeking tube and iron shard,
All valiant dust that builds on dust,
   And guarding, calls not Thee to guard,
For frantic boast and foolish word –
Thy mercy on Thy People, Lord!

'FOR ALL WE HAVE AND ARE'

1914

For all we have and are,
For all our children's fate,
Stand up and take the war.
The Hun is at the gate!
Our world has passed away,
In wantonness o'erthrown.
There is nothing left to-day
But steel and fire and stone!
    Though all we knew depart,
    The old Commandments stand: –
    'In courage keep your heart,
    In strength lift up your hand.'

Once more we hear the word
That sickened earth of old: –
'No law except the Sword
Unsheathed and uncontrolled.'
Once more it knits mankind,
Once more the nations go
To meet and break and bind
A crazed and driven foe.

Comfort, content, delight,
The ages' slow-bought gain,
They shrivelled in a night.
Only ourselves remain
To face the naked days
In silent fortitude,
Through perils and dismays
Renewed and re-renewed.

Though all we made depart,
The old Commandments stand: –
'In patience keep your heart,
In strength lift up your hand.'

No easy hope or lies
Shall bring us to our goal,
But iron sacrifice
Of body, will, and soul.
There is but one task for all –
One life for each to give.
What stands if Freedom fall?
Who dies if England live?

THE THREE-DECKER
1894

'The three-volume novel is extinct.'

Full thirty foot she towered from waterline to rail.
It took a watch to steer her, and a week to shorten sail;
But, spite all modern notions, I've found her first and best –
The only certain packet for the Islands of the Blest.

Fair held the breeze behind us – 'twas warm with lovers' prayers.
We'd stolen wills for ballast and a crew of missing heirs.
They shipped as Able Bastards till the Wicked Nurse confessed,
And they worked the old three-decker to the Islands of the Blest.

By ways no gaze could follow, a course unspoiled of Cook,
Per Fancy, fleetest in man, our titled berths we took,
With maids of matchless beauty and parentage unguessed,
And a Church of England parson for the Islands of the Blest.

We asked no social questions – we pumped no hidden shame –
We never talked obstetrics when the Little Stranger came:
We left the Lord in Heaven, we left the fiends in Hell.
We weren't exactly Yussufs, but – Zuleika didn't tell.

No moral doubt assailed us, so when the port we neared,
The villain had his flogging at the gangway, and we cheered.
'Twas fiddle in the foc's'le – 'twas garlands on the mast,
For every one got married, and I went ashore at last.

I left 'em all in couples a-kissing on the decks.
I left the lovers loving and the parents signing cheques.
In endless English comfort, by county-folk caressed,
I left the old three-decker at the Islands of the Blest! . . .

That route is barred to steamers: you'll never lift again
Our purple-painted headlands or the lordly keeps of Spain.
They're just beyond your skyline, howe'er so far you cruise
In a ram-you-damn-you liner with a brace of bucking screws.

Swing round your aching searchlight – 'twill show no haven's peace.
Ay, blow your shrieking sirens at the deaf, grey-bearded seas!
Boom out the dripping oil-bags to skin the deep's unrest –
And you aren't one knot the nearer to the Islands of the Blest.

But when you're threshing, crippled, with broken bridge and rail,
At a drogue of dead convictions to hold you head to gale,
Calm as the Flying Dutchman, from truck to taffrail dressed,
You'll see the old three-decker for the Islands of the Blest.

You'll see her tiering canvas in sheeted silver spread;
You'll hear the long-drawn thunder 'neath her leaping figurehead;
While far, so far above you, her tall poop-lanterns shine
Unvexed by wind or weather like the candles round a shrine!

Hull down – hull down and under – she dwindles to a speck,
With noise of pleasant music and dancing on her deck.
All's well – all's well aboard her – she's left you far behind,
With a scent of old-world roses through the fog that ties you blind.

Her crews are babes or madmen? Her port is all to make?
You're manned by Truth and Science, and you steam for steaming's
sake?
Well, tinker up your engines – you know your business best –
She's taking tired people to the Islands of the Blest!

THE RHYME OF THE THREE CAPTAINS
1890

[This ballad appears to refer to one of the exploits of the notorious Paul Jones, an American pirate. It is founded on fact.][1]

. . . At the close of a winter day,
Their anchors down, by London town, the Three Great Captains lay;
And one was Admiral of the North from Solway Firth to Skye,
And one was Lord of the Wessex coast and all the lands thereby,
And one was Master of the Thames from Limehouse to Blackwall,
And he was Chaplain of the Fleet – the bravest of them all.
Their good guns guarded their great grey sides that were thirty foot in the sheer,
When there came a certain trading brig with news of a privateer.
Her rigging was rough with the clotted drift that drives in a Northern breeze,
Her sides were clogged with the lazy weed that spawns in the Eastern seas.
Light she rode in the rude tide-rip, to left and right she rolled,
And the skipper sat on the scuttle-butt and stared at an empty hold.
'I ha' paid Port dues for your Law,' quoth he, 'and where is the Law ye boast

[1] The ballad does refer to fact, but not to Paul Jones. The pirate is the American publisher who pirated Kipling's work without payment, and the Three Captains are Sir Walter Besant, Thomas Hardy and William Black, who defended him, to Kipling's chagrin. See Charles Carrington, *Rudyard Kipling*, Macmillan, 1955, Pelican, 1970. (Ed.)

'If I sail unscathed from a heathen port to be robbed on a Christian coast?
'Ye have smoked the hives of the Laccadives as we burn the lice in a bunk,
'We tack not now for a Gallang prow or a plunging Pei-ho junk;
'I had no fear but the seas were clear as far as a sail might fare
'Till I met with a lime-washed Yankee brig that rode off Finisterre.
'There were canvas blinds to his bow-gun ports to screen the weight he bore,
'And the signals ran for a merchantman from Sandy Hook to the Nore.
'He would not fly the Rovers' flag – the bloody or the black,
'But now he floated the Gridiron and now he flaunted the Jack.
'He spoke of the Law as he crimped my crew – he swore it was only a loan;
'But when I would ask for my own again, he swore it was none of my own.
'He has taken my little parrakeets that nest beneath the Line,
'He has stripped my rails of the shaddock-frails and the green unripened pine.
'He has taken my bale of dammer and spice I won beyond the seas,
'He has taken my grinning heathen gods – and what should he want o' these?
'My foremast would not mend his boom, my deck-house patch his boats;
'He has whittled the two, this Yank Yahoo, to peddle for shoe-peg oats.
'I could not fight for the failing light and a rough beam-sea beside,
'But I hulled him once for a clumsy crimp and twice because he lied.
'Had I had guns (as I had goods) to work my Christian harm,
'I had run him up from his quarter-deck to trade with his own yard-arm;

'I had nailed his ears to my capstan-head, and ripped them off with a saw,
'And soused them in the bilgewater, and served them to him raw;
'I had flung him blind in a rudderless boat to rot in the rocking dark,
'I had towed him aft of his own craft, a bait for his brother shark;
'I had lapped him round with cocoa-husk, and drenched him with the oil,
'And lashed him fast to his own mast to blaze above my spoil;
'I had stripped his hide for my hammock-side, and tasselled his beard in the mesh,
'And spitted his crew on the live bamboo that grows through the gangrened flesh;
'I had hove him down by the mangroves brown, where the mud-reef sucks and draws,
'Moored by the heel to his own keel to wait for the land-crab's claws.
'He is lazar within and lime without; ye can nose him far enow,
'For he carries the taint of a musky ship – the reek of the slaver's dhow.'

The skipper looked at the tiering guns and the bulwarks tall and cold,
And the Captains Three full courteously peered down at the gutted hold,
And the Captains Three called courteously from deck to scuttle-butt:–
'Good Sir, we ha' dealt with that merchantman or ever your teeth were cut.
'Your words be words of a lawless race, and the Law it standeth thus:
'He comes of a race that have never a Law, and he never has boarded us.
'We ha' sold him canvas and rope and spar – we know that his price is fair,
'And we know that he weeps for the lack of a Law as he rides off Finisterre.

'And since he is damned for a gallows-thief by you and better than you,
'We hold it meet that the English fleet should know that we hold him true.'
The skipper called to the tall taffrail: – 'And what is that to me?
'Did ever you hear of a Yankee brig that rifled a Seventy-three?
'Do I loom so large from your quarter-deck that I lift like a ship o' the Line?
'He has learned to run from a shotted gun and harry such craft as mine.
'There is never a law on the Cocos Keys, to hold a white man in,
'But we do not steal the niggers' meal, for that is a nigger's sin.
'Must he have his Law as a quid to chaw, or laid in brass on his wheel?
'Does he steal with tears when he buccaneers? 'Fore Gad, then, why does he steal?'
The skipper bit on a deep-sea word, and the word it was not sweet,
For he could see the Captains Three had signalled to the Fleet.
But three and two, in white and blue, the whimpering flags began :–
'We have heard a tale of a – foreign sail, but he is a merchantman.'
The skipper peered beneath his palm and swore by the Great Horn Spoon: –
''Fore Gad, the Chaplain of the Fleet would bless my picaroon!'
By two and three the flags blew free to lash the laughing air: –
'We have sold our spars to the merchantman – we know that his price is fair.'
The skipper winked his Western eye, and swore by a China storm: –
'They ha' rigged him a Joseph's jury-coat to keep his honour warm.'
The halliards twanged against the tops, the bunting bellied broad,
The skipper spat in the empty hold and mourned for a wasted cord.
Masthead – masthead, the signal sped by the line o' the British craft:
The skipper called to his Lascar crew, and put her about and laughed: –

'It's mainsail haul, my bully boys all – we'll out to the seas again –
'Ere they set us to paint their pirate saint, or scrub at his grapnel-chain.
'It's fore-sheet free, with her head to the sea, and the swing of the unbought brine –
'We'll make no sport in an English court till we come as a ship o' the Line:
'Till we come as a ship o' the Line, my lads, of thirty foot in the sheer,
'Lifting again from the outer main with news of a privateer;
'Flying his pluck at our mizzen-truck for weft of Admiralty,
'Heaving his head for our dipsy-lead in sign that we keep the sea.
'Then fore-sheet home as she lifts to the foam – we stand on the outward tack,
'We are paid in the coin of the white man's trade – the bezant is hard, ay, and black.
'The frigate-bird shall carry my word to the Kling and the Orang-Laut
'How a man may sail from a heathen coast to be robbed in a Christian port;
'How a man may be robbed in Christian port while Three Great Captains there
'Shall dip their flag to a slaver's rag – to show that his trade is fair!'

THE CONUNDRUM OF THE WORKSHOPS
1890

When the flush of a new-born sun fell first on Eden's green and gold,
Our father Adam sat under the Tree and scratched with a stick in the mould;
And the first rude sketch that the world had seen was joy to his mighty heart,
Till the Devil whispered behind the leaves, 'It's pretty, but is it Art?'

Wherefore he called to his wife, and fled to fashion his work anew –
The first of his race who cared a fig for the first, most dread review;
And he left his lore to the use of his sons – and that was a glorious gain
When the Devil chuckled 'Is it Art?' in the ear of the branded Cain.

They builded a tower to shiver the sky and wrench the stars apart,
Till the Devil grunted behind the bricks: 'It's striking, but is it Art?'
The stone was dropped at the quarry-side and the idle derrick swung,
While each man talked of the aims of Art, and each in an alien tongue.

They fought and they talked in the North and the South; they talked and they fought in the West,
Till the waters rose on the pitiful land, and the poor Red Clay had rest –
Had rest till that dank blank-canvas dawn when the Dove was preened to start,
And the Devil bubbled below the keel: 'It's human, but is it Art?'

The tale is as old as the Eden Tree – and new as the new-cut tooth –
For each man knows ere his lip-thatch grows he is master of Art and
Truth;
And each man hears as the twilight nears, to the beat of his dying
heart,
The Devil drum on the darkened pane: 'You did it, but was it Art?'

We have learned to whittle the Eden Tree to the shape of a surplice-
peg,
We have learned to bottle our parents twain in the yelk of an addled
egg,
We know that the tail must wag the dog, for the horse is drawn by
the cart;
But the Devil whoops, as he whooped of old: 'It's clever, but is it
Art?'

When the flicker of London sun falls faint on the Club-room's green
and gold,
The sons of Adam sit them down and scratch with their pens in the
mould –
They scratch with their pens in the mould of their graves, and the
ink and the anguish start,
For the Devil mutters behind the leaves: 'It's pretty, but is it Art?'

Now, if we could win to the Eden Tree where the Four Great
Rivers flow,
And the Wreath of Eve is red on the turf as she left it long ago,
And if we could come when the sentry slept and softly scurry
through,
By the favour of God we might know as much – as our father Adam
knew!

IN THE NEOLITHIC AGE
1895

In the Neolithic Age savage warfare did I wage
For food and fame and woolly horses' pelt.
I was singer to my clan in that dim, red Dawn of Man,
And I sang of all we fought and feared and felt.

Yea, I sang as now I sing, when the Prehistoric spring
Made the piled Biscayan ice-pack split and shove;
And the troll and gnome and dwerg, and the Gods of Cliff and Berg
Were about me and beneath me and above.

But a rival, of Solutré, told the tribe my style was *outré* –
'Neath a tomahawk, of diorite, he fell.
And I left my views on Art, barbed and tanged, below the heart
Of a mammothistic etcher at Grenelle.

Then I stripped them, scalp from skull, and my hunting-dogs fed full,
And their teeth I threaded neatly on a thong;
And I wiped my mouth and said, 'It is well that they are dead,
'For I know my work is right and theirs was wrong.'

But my Totem saw the shame; from his ridgepole-shrine he came,
And he told me in a vision of the night: –
'There are nine and sixty ways of constructing tribal lays,
'And every single one of them is right!'

. . .

Then the silence closed upon me till They put new clothing on me
Of whiter, weaker flesh and bone more frail;
And I stepped beneath Time's finger, once again a tribal singer,
And a minor poet certified by Traill!

Still they skirmish to and fro, men my messmates on the snow,
When we headed off the aurochs turn for turn;
When the rich Allobrogenses never kept amanuenses,
And our only plots were piled in lakes at Berne.

Still a cultured Christian age sees us scuffle, squeak, and rage,
Still we pinch and slap and jabber, scratch and dirk;
Still we let our business slide – as we dropped the half-dressed hide –
To show a fellow-savage how to work.

Still the world is wondrous large, – seven seas from marge to marge –
And it holds a vast of various kinds of man;
And the wildest dreams of Kew are the facts of Khatmandhu,
And the crimes of Clapham chaste in Martaban.

Here's my wisdom for your use, as I learned it when the moose
And the reindeer roamed where Paris roars to-night: –
'*There are nine and sixty ways of constructing tribal lays,*
'*And – every – single – one – of – them – is – right!*'

'WHEN 'OMER SMOTE 'IS BLOOMIN' LYRE'

(Introduction to *The Barrack-room Ballads* in *The Seven Seas*

When 'Omer smote 'is bloomin' lyre,
He'd 'eard men sing by land an' sea;
An' what he thought 'e might require,
'E went an' took – the same as me!

The market-girls an' fishermen,
The shepherds an' the sailors, too,
They 'eard old songs turn up again,
But kep' it quiet – same as you!

They knew 'e stole; 'e knew they knowed.
They didn't tell, nor make a fuss,
But winked at 'Omer down the road,
An' 'e winked back – the same as us!

THE FEMALE OF THE SPECIES
1911

When the Himalayan peasant meets the he-bear in his pride,
He shouts to scare the monster, who will often turn aside.
But the she-bear thus accosted rends the peasant tooth and nail.
For the female of the species is more deadly than the male.

When Nag the basking cobra hears the careless foot of man,
He will sometimes wriggle sideways and avoid it if he can.
But his mate makes no such motion where she camps beside the trail.
For the female of the species is more deadly than the male.

When the early Jesuit fathers preached to Hurons and Choctaws,
They prayed to be delivered from the vengeance of the squaws.
'Twas the women, not the warriors, turned those stark enthusiasts pale.
For the female of the species is more deadly than the male.

Man's timid heart is bursting with the things he must not say,
For the Woman that God gave him isn't his to give away;
But when hunter meets with husband, each confirms the other's tale –
The female of the species is more deadly than the male.

Man, a bear in most relations – worm and savage otherwise, –
Man propounds negotiations, Man accepts the compromise.
Very rarely will he squarely push the logic of a fact
To its ultimate conclusion in unmitigated act.

Fear, or foolishness, impels him, ere he lay the wicked low,
To concede some form of trial even to his fiercest foe.
Mirth obscene diverts his anger – Doubt and Pity oft perplex
Him in dealing with an issue – to the scandal of The Sex!

But the Woman that God gave him, every fibre of her frame
Proves her launched for one sole issue, armed and engined for the
same;
And to serve that single issue, lest the generations fail,
The female of the species must be deadlier than the male.

She who faces Death by torture for each life beneath her breast
May not deal in doubt or pity – must not swerve for fact or jest.
These be purely male diversions – not in these her honour dwells.
She the Other Law we live by, is that Law and nothing else.

She can bring no more to living than the powers that make her great
As the Mother of the Infant and the Mistress of the Mate.
And when Babe and Man are lacking and she strides unclaimed to
claim
Her right as femme (and baron), her equipment is the same.

She is wedded to convictions – in default of grosser ties;
Her contentions are her children, Heaven help him who denies! –
He will meet no suave discussion, but the instant, white-hot, wild,
Wakened female of the species warring as for spouse and child.

Unprovoked and awful charges – even so the she-bear fights,
Speech that drips, corrodes, and poisons – even so the cobra bites,
Scientific vivisection of one nerve till it is raw
And the victim writhes in anguish – like the Jesuit with the squaw!

So it comes that Man, the coward, when he gathers to confer
With his fellow-braves in council, dare not leave a place for her
Where, at war with Life and Conscience, he uplifts his erring hands
To some God of Abstract Justice – which no woman understands.

And Man knows it! Knows, moreover, that the Woman that God
gave him
Must command but may not govern – shall enthral but not enslave
him.
And *She* knows, because She warns him, and Her instincts never fail,
That the Female of Her Species is more deadly than the Male.

THE EXPLANATION
1890

Love and Death once ceased their strife
At the Tavern of Man's Life.
Called for wine, and threw – alas! –
Each his quiver on the grass.
When the bout was o'er they found
Mingled arrows strewed the ground.
Hastily they gathered then
Each the loves and lives of men.
Ah, the fateful dawn deceived!
Mingled arrows each one sheaved.
Death's dread armoury was stored
With the shafts he most abhorred;
Love's light quiver groaned beneath
Venom-headed darts of Death.
Thus it was they wrought our woe
At the Tavern long ago.
Tell me, do our masters know,
Loosing blindly as they fly,
Old men love while young men die?

THE KING
1894

'Farewell, Romance!' the Cave-men said;
 'With bone well carved He went away.
'Flint arms the ignoble arrowhead,
 'And jasper tips the spear to-day.
'Changed are the Gods of Hunt and Dance,
'And He with these. Farewell, Romance!'

'Farewell, Romance!' the Lake-folk sighed;
 'We lift the weight of flatling years;
'The caverns of the mountain-side
 'Hold Him who scorns our hutted piers.
'Lost hills whereby we dare not dwell,
'Guard ye His rest. Romance, Farewell!'

'Farewell, Romance!' the Soldier spoke;
 'By sleight of sword we may not win,
'But scuffle 'mid uncleanly smoke
 'Of arquebus and culverin.
'Honour is lost, and none may tell
'Who paid good blows. Romance, farewell!'

'Farewell, Romance!' the Traders cried;
 'Our keels have lain with every sea.
'The dull-returning wind and tide
 'Heave up the wharf where we would be;
'The known and noted breezes swell
'Our trudging sails. Romance, farewell!'

'Good-bye, Romance!' the Skipper said;
  'He vanished with the coal we burn.
'Our dial marks full-steam ahead,
  'Our speed is timed to half a turn.
'Sure as the ferried barge we ply
'"Twixt port and port. Romance, good-bye!'

'Romance!' the season-tickets mourn,
  '*He* never ran to catch His train,
'But passed with coach and guard and horn –
  'And left the local – late again!
'Confound Romance!' . . . And all unseen
Romance brought up the nine-fifteen.

His hand was on the lever laid,
  His oil-can soothed the worrying cranks,
His whistle waked the snowbound grade,
  His fog-horn cut the reeking Banks;
By dock and deep and mine and mill
The Boy-god reckless laboured still!

Robed, crowned and throned, He wove His spell,
  Where heart-blood beat or hearth-smoke curled,
With unconsidered miracle,
  Hedged in a backward-gazing world:
Then taught His chosen bard to say:
'Our King was with us – yesterday!'

THE SONS OF MARTHA
1907

The Sons of Mary seldom bother, for they have inherited that good part;
But the Sons of Martha favour their Mother of the careful soul and the troubled heart.
And because she lost her temper once, and because she was rude to the Lord her Guest,
Her Sons must wait upon Mary's Sons, world without end, reprieve, or rest.

It is their care in all the ages to take the buffer and cushion the shock.
It is their care that the gear engages; it is their care that the switches lock.
It is their care that the wheels run truly; it is their care to embark and entrain,
Tally, transport, and deliver duly the Sons of Mary by land and main.

They say to mountains, 'Be ye removèd.' They say to the lesser floods, 'Be dry.'
Under their rods are the rocks reprovèd – they are not afraid of that which is high.
Then do the hill-tops shake to the summit – then is the bed of the deep laid bare,
That the Sons of Mary may overcome it, pleasantly sleeping and unaware.

They finger death at their gloves' end where they piece and repiece the living wires.

He rears against the gates they tend: they feed him hungry behind
 their fires.
Early at dawn, ere men see clear, they stumble into his terrible
 stall,
And hale him forth like a haltered steer, and goad and turn him till
 evenfall.

To these from birth is Belief forbidden; from these till death is
 Relief afar.
They are concerned with matters hidden – under the earthline their
 altars are –
The secret fountains to follow up, waters withdrawn to restore to the
 mouth,
And gather the floods as in a cup, and pour them again at a city's
 drouth.

They do not preach that their God will rouse them a little before the
 nuts work loose.
They do not teach that His Pity allows them to drop their job when
 they dam'-well choose.
As in the thronged and the lighted ways, so in the dark and the desert
 they stand,
Wary and watchful all their days that their brethren's days may be
 long in the land.

Raise ye the stone or cleave the wood to make a path more fair or
 flat –
Lo, it is black already with blood some Son of Martha spilled for
 that!
Not as a ladder from earth to Heaven, not as a witness to any creed,
But simple service simply given to his own kind in their common
 need.

And the Sons of Mary smile and are blessèd – they know the Angels
are on their side.
They know in them is the Grace confessèd, and for them are the
Mercies multiplied.
They sit at the Feet – they hear the Word – they see how truly the
Promise runs.
They have cast their burden upon the Lord, and – the Lord He lays
it on Martha's Sons!

'BOBS'
1898
(Field-Marshal Lord Roberts of Kandahar: died in France 1914)

There's a little red-faced man,
Which is Bobs,
Rides the tallest 'orse 'e can –
Our Bobs.
If it bucks or kicks or rears,
'E can sit for twenty years
With a smile round both 'is ears –
Can't yer, Bobs?

Then 'ere's to Bobs Bahadur – little Bobs, Bobs, Bobs!
'E's our pukka Kandaharder –
Fightin' Bobs, Bobs, Bobs!
'E's the Dook of *Aggy Chel*;[1]
'E's the man that done us well,
An' we'll follow 'im to 'ell –
Won't we, Bobs?

If a limber's slipped a trace,
'Ook on Bobs.
If a marker's lost 'is place,
Dress by Bobs.
For 'e's eyes all up 'is coat,
An' a bugle in 'is throat,
An' you will not play the goat
Under Bobs.

[1] Get ahead.

'E's a little down on drink,
        Chaplain Bobs;
But it keeps us outer Clink –
        Don't it, Bobs?
So we will not complain
Tho' 'e's water on the brain,
If 'e leads us straight again –
        Blue-light[1] Bobs.

If you stood 'im on 'is head,
        Father Bobs,
You could spill a quart of lead
        Outer Bobs.
'E's been at it thirty years,
An-amassin' souveneers
In the way o' slugs an' spears –
        Ain't yer, Bobs?

What 'e does not know o' war,
        Gen'ral Bobs,
You can arst the shop next door –
        Can't they, Bobs?
Oh, 'e's little but he's wise,
'E's a terror for 'is size,
An' – *'e – does – not – advertise* –
        Do yer, Bobs?

Now they've made a bloomin' Lord
        Outer Bobs,
Which was but 'is fair reward –
        Weren't it, Bobs?

[1] Temperance.

So 'e'll wear a coronet
Where 'is 'elmet used to set;
But we know you won't forget –
        Will yer, Bobs?

Then 'ere's to Bobs Bahadur – little Bobs, Bobs, Bobs,
Pocket-Wellin'ton an' *arder*[1] –
        Fightin' Bobs, Bobs, Bobs!
This ain't no bloomin' ode,
But you've 'elped the soldier's load,
An' for benefits bestowed,
        Bless yer, Bobs!

[1] And a half.

DANNY DEEVER

'What are the bugles blowin' for?' said Files-on-Parade.
'To turn you out, to turn you out,' the Colour-Sergeant said.
'What makes you look so white, so white?' said Files-on-Parade.
'I'm dreadin' what I've got to watch,' the Colour-Sergeant said.
For they're hangin' Danny Deever, you can hear the Dead March play,
The Regiment's in 'ollow square – they're hangin' him to-day;
They've taken of his buttons off an' cut his stripes away,
An' they're hangin' Danny Deever in the mornin'.

'What makes the rear-rank breathe so 'ard?' said Files-on-Parade.
'It's bitter cold, it's bitter cold,' the Colour-Sergeant said.
'What makes that front-rank man fall down?' said Files-on-Parade.
'A touch o' sun, a touch o' sun,' the Colour-Sergeant said.
They are hangin' Danny Deever, they are marchin' of 'im round,
They 'ave 'alted Danny Deever by 'is coffin on the ground;
An' 'e'll swing in 'arf a minute for a sneakin' shootin' hound –
O they're hangin' Danny Deever in the mornin'!

''Is cot was right-'and cot to mine,' said Files-on-Parade.
''E's sleepin' out an' far to-night,' the Colour-Sergeant said.
'I've drunk 'is beer a score o' times,' said Files-on-Parade.
''E's drinkin' bitter beer alone,' the Colour-Sergeant said.
They are hangin' Danny Deever, you must mark 'im to 'is place,
For 'e shot a comrade sleepin' – you must look 'im in the face;
Nine 'undred of 'is county an' the Regiment's disgrace,
While they're hangin' Danny Deever in the mornin'.

'What's that so black agin the sun?' said Files-on-Parade.
'It's Danny fightin' 'ard for life,' the Colour-Sergeant said.

'What's that that whimpers over'ead?' said Files-on-Parade.
'It's Danny's soul that's passin' now,' the Colour-Sergeant said.
For they're done with Danny Deever, you can 'ear the quickstep play,
The Regiment's in column, an' they're marchin' us away;
Ho! the young recruits are shakin', an' they'll want their beer to-day,
After hangin' Danny Deever in the mornin'!

TOMMY

I went into a public-'ouse to get a pint o' beer,
The publican 'e up an' sez, 'We serve no red-coats here.'
The girls be'ind the bar they laughed an' giggled fit to die,
I outs into the street again an' to myself sez I:
O it's Tommy this, an' Tommy that, an' 'Tommy, go away';
But it's 'Thank you, Mister Atkins,' when the band begins to play –
The band begins to play, my boys, the band begins to play,
O it's 'Thank you, Mister Atkins,' when the band begins to play.

I went into a theatre as sober as could be,
They gave a drunk civilian room, but 'adn't none for me;
They sent me to the gallery or round the music-'alls,
But when it comes to fightin', Lord! they'll shove me in the stalls!
For it's Tommy this, an' Tommy that, an' 'Tommy, wait outside';
But it's 'Special train for Atkins' when the trooper's on the tide –
The troopship's on the tide, my boys, the troopship's on the tide,
O it's 'Special train for Atkins' when the trooper's on the tide.

Yes, makin' mock o' uniforms that guard you while you sleep
Is cheaper than them uniforms, an' they're starvation cheap;
An' hustlin' drunken soldiers when they're goin' large a bit
Is five times better business than paradin' in full kit.

Then it's Tommy this, an' Tommy that, an' 'Tommy, 'ow's yer soul?'
But it's 'Thin red line of 'eroes' when the drums begin to roll –
The drums begin to roll, my boys, the drums begin to roll,
O it's 'Thin red line of 'eroes' when the drums begin to roll.

We aren't no thin red 'eroes, nor we aren't no blackguards too,
But single men in barricks, most remarkable like you;
An' if sometimes our conduck isn't all your fancy paints,
Why, single men in barricks don't grow into plaster saints;
While it's Tommy this, an' Tommy that, an' 'Tommy, fall be'ind,'
But it's 'Please to walk in front, sir,' when there's trouble in the wind –
There's trouble in the wind, my boys, there's trouble in the wind,
O it's 'Please to walk in front, sir,' when there's trouble in the wind.

You talk o' better food for us, an' schools, an' fires, an' all:
We'll wait for extry rations if you treat us rational.
Don't mess about the cook-room slops, but prove it to our face
The Widow's Uniform is not the soldier-man's disgrace.
For it's Tommy this, an' Tommy that, an' 'Chuck him out, the brute!'
But it's 'Saviour of 'is country' when the guns begin to shoot;
An' it's Tommy this, an' Tommy that, an' anything you please;
An' Tommy ain't a bloomin' fool – you bet that Tommy sees!

'FUZZY-WUZZY'

(Soudan Expeditionary Force.
Early Campaigns)

We've fought with many men acrost the seas,
  An' some of 'em was brave an' some was not:
The Paythan an' the Zulu an' Burmese;
  But the Fuzzy was the finest o' the lot.
We never got a ha'porth's change of 'im:
  'E squatted in the scrub an' 'ocked our 'orses,
'E cut our sentries up at Sua*kim*,
  An' 'e played the cat an' banjo with our forces.
    So 'ere's *to* you, Fuzzy-Wuzzy, at your 'ome in the Soudan;
    You're a pore benighted 'eathen but a first-class fightin' man;
    We gives you your certificate, an' if you want it signed
    We'll come an' 'ave a romp with you whenever you're inclined.

We took our chanst among the Kyber 'ills,
  The Boers knocked us silly at a mile,
The Burman give us Irriwaddy chills,
  An' a Zulu *impi* dished us up in style:
But all we ever got from such as they
  Was pop to what the Fuzzy made us swaller;
We 'eld our bloomin' own, the papers say,
  But man for man the Fuzzy knocked us 'oller.
    Then 'ere's *to* you, Fuzzy-Wuzzy, an' the missis and the kid;
    Our orders was to break you, an' of course we went an' did.
    We sloshed you with Martinis, an' it wasn't 'ardly fair;
    But for all the odds agin' you, Fuzzy-Wuz, you broke the square.

'E 'asn't got no papers of 'is own,
  'E 'asn't got no medals nor rewards,
So *we* must certify the skill 'e's shown
  In usin' of 'is long two-'anded swords:
When 'e's 'oppin' in an' out among the bush
  With 'is coffin-'eaded shield an' shovel-spear,
An 'appy day with Fuzzy on the rush
  Will last an 'ealthy Tommy for a year.
    So 'ere's *to* you, Fuzzy-Wuzzy, an' your friends which are no more,
    If we 'adn't lost some messmates we would 'elp you to deplore.
    But give an' take's the gospel, an' we'll call the bargain fair,
    For if you 'ave lost more than us, you crumpled up the square!

'E rushes at the smoke when we let drive,
  An', before we know, 'e's 'ackin' at our 'ead;
'E's all 'ot sand an' ginger when alive,
  An' 'e's generally shammin' when 'e's dead.
'E's a daisy, 'e's a ducky, 'e's a lamb!
  'E's a injia-rubber idiot on the spree,
'E's the on'y thing that doesn't give a damn
  For a Regiment o' British Infantree!
    So 'ere's *to* you, Fuzzy-Wuzzy, at your 'ome in the Soudan;
    You're a pore benighted 'eathen but a first-class fightin' man;
    An' 'ere's *to* you, Fuzzy-Wuzzy, with your 'ayrick 'ead of 'air –
    You big black boundin' beggar – for you broke a British square!

CELLS

I've a head like a concertina, I've a tongue like a button-stick,
I've a mouth like an old potato, and I'm more than a little sick,
But I've had my fun o' the Corp'ral's Guard; I've made the cinders fly.
And I'm here in the Clink for a thundering drink and blacking the Corporal's eye.

With a second-hand overcoat under my head,
And a beautiful view of the yard,
O it's pack-drill for me and a fortnight's C. B.
For 'drunk and resisting the Guard'!
Mad drunk and resisting the Guard –
'Strewth, but I socked it them hard!
So it's pack-drill for me and a fortnight's C.B.
For 'drunk and resisting the Guard'.

I started o' canteen porter, I finished o' canteen beer,
But a dose o' gin that a mate slipped in, it was that that brought me here.
'Twas that and an extry double Guard that rubbed my nose in the dirt –
But I fell away with the Corp'ral's stock and the best of the Corp'ral's shirt.

I left my cap in a public-house, my boots in the public road,
And Lord knows where – and I don't care – my belt and my tunic goed.
They'll stop my pay, they'll cut away the stripes I used to wear,
But I left my mark on the Corp'ral's face, and I think he'll keep it there!

My wife she cries on the barrack-gate, my kid in the barrack-yard.
It ain't that I mind the Ord'ly-room – it's *that* that cuts so hard.
I'll take my oath before them both that I will sure abstain,
But as soon as I'm in with a mate and gin, I know I'll do it again!

With a second-hand overcoat under my head,
And a beautiful view of the yard,
Yes, it's pack-drill for me and a fortnight's C.B.
For 'drunk and resisting the Guard'!
Mad drunk and resisting the Guard –
'Strewth, but I socked it them hard!
So it's pack-drill for me and a fortnight's C.B.
For 'drunk and resisting the Guard'.

GUNGA DIN

You may talk o' gin and beer
When you're quartered safe out 'ere,
An' you're sent to penny-fights an' Aldershot it;
But when it comes to slaughter
You will do your work on water,
An' you'll lick the bloomin' boots of 'im that's got it.
Now in Injia's sunny clime,
Where I used to spend my time
A-servin' of 'Er Majesty the Queen,
Of all them blackfaced crew
The finest man I knew
Was our regimental bhisti, Gunga Din.
    He was 'Din! Din! Din!
  'You limpin' lump o' brick-dust, Gunga Din!
    'Hi! Slippy *hitherao!*
    'Water, get it! *Panee lao*,[1]
  'You squidgy-nosed old idol, Gunga Din.'

The uniform 'e wore
Was nothin' much before,
An' rather less than 'arf o' that be'ind,
For a piece o' twisty rag
An' a goatskin water-bag
Was all the field-equipment 'e could find.
When the sweatin' troop-train lay
In a sidin' through the day,
Where the 'eat would make your bloomin' eyebrows crawl,
We shouted 'Harry By!'[2]

[1] Bring water swiftly. [2] O brother.

Till our throats were bricky-dry,
Then we wopped 'im 'cause 'e couldn't serve us all.
    It was 'Din! Din! Din!
  'You 'eathen, where the mischief 'ave you been?
    'You put some *juldee*[1] in it
    'Or I'll *marrow*[2] you this minute
  'If you don't fill up my helmet, Gunga Din!'

'E would dot an' carry one
Till the longest day was done;
An' 'e didn't seem to know the use o' fear.
If we charged or broke or cut,
You could bet your bloomin' nut,
'E'd be waitin' fifty paces right flank rear.
With 'is mussick[3] on 'is back,
'E would skip with our attack,
An' watch us till the bugles made 'Retire',
An' for all 'is dirty 'ide
'E was white, clear white, inside
When 'e went to tend the wounded under fire!
    It was 'Din! Din! Din!'
  With the bullets kickin' dust-spots on the green.
    When the cartridges ran out,
    You could hear the front-ranks shout,
  'Hi! ammunition-mules an' Gunga Din!'

I shan't forgit the night
When I dropped be'ind the fight
With a bullet where my belt-plate should 'a' been.
I was chokin' mad with thirst,
An' the man that spied me first
Was our good old grinnin', gruntin' Gunga Din.

[1] Be quick. [2] Hit. [3] Water-skin.

'E lifted up my 'ead,
An' he plugged me where I bled,
An' 'e guv me 'arf-a-pint o' water green.
It was crawlin' and it stunk,
But of all the drinks I've drunk,
I'm gratefullest to one from Gunga Din.
    It was 'Din! Din! Din!
  ''Ere's a beggar with a bullet through 'is spleen;
      ''E's chawin' up the ground,
      'An' 'e's kickin' all around:
  'For Gawd's sake git the water, Gunga Din!'

'E carried me away
To where a dooli lay,
An' a bullet come an' drilled the beggar clean.
'E put me safe inside,
An' just before 'e died,
'I 'ope you liked your drink,' sez Gunga Din.
So I'll meet 'im later on
At the place where 'e is gone –
Where it's always double drill and no canteen.
'E'll be squattin' on the coals
Givin' drink to poor damned souls,
An' I'll get a swig in hell from Gunga Din!
    Yes, Din! Din! Din!
  You Lazarushian-leather Gunga Din!
    Though I've belted you and flayed you,
    By the livin' Gawd that made you,
  You're a better man than I am, Gunga Din!

THE WIDOW AT WINDSOR

'Ave you 'eard o' the Widow at Windsor
  With a hairy gold crown on 'er 'ead?
She 'as ships on the foam – she 'as millions at 'ome,
  An' she pays us poor beggars in red.
    (Ow, poor beggars in red!)
There's 'er nick on the cavalry 'orses,
  There's 'er mark on the medical stores –
An' 'er troopers you'll find with a fair wind be'ind
  That takes us to various wars.
    (Poor beggars! – barbarious wars!)
      Then 'ere's to the Widow at Windsor,
        An' 'ere's to the stores an' the guns,
      The men an' the 'orses what makes up the forces
        O' Missis Victorier's sons.
      (Poor beggars! Victorier's sons!)

Walk wide o' the Widow at Windsor,
  For 'alf o' Creation she owns:
We 'ave bought 'er the same with the sword an' the flame,
  An' we've salted it down with our bones.
    (Poor beggars! – it's blue with our bones!)
Hands off o' the sons o' the Widow,
  Hands off o' the goods in 'er shop,
For the Kings must come down an' the Emperors frown
  When the Widow at Windsor says 'Stop!'
    (Poor beggars! – we're sent to say 'Stop!')
      Then 'ere's to the Lodge o' the Widow,
        From the Pole to the Tropics it runs –

To the Lodge that we tile with the rank an' the file,
An' open in form with the guns.
(Poor beggars! – it's always they guns!)

We 'ave 'eard o' the Widow at Windsor,
It's safest to leave 'er alone:
For 'er sentries we stand by the sea an' the land
Wherever the bugles are blown.
(Poor beggars! – an' don't we get blown!)
Take 'old o' the Wings o' the Mornin',
An' flop round the earth till you're dead;
But you won't get away from the tune that they play
To the bloomin' old rag over'ead.
(Poor beggars! – it's 'ot over'ead!)
Then 'ere's to the Sons o' the Widow,
Wherever, 'owever they roam.
'Ere's all they desire, an' if they require
A speedy return to their 'ome.
(Poor beggars! – they'll never see 'ome!)

BELTS

There was a row in Silver Street that's near to Dublin Quay,
Between an Irish regiment an' English cavalree;
It started at Revelly an' it lasted on till dark:
The first man dropped at Harrison's, the last forninst the
   Park.
      For it was: – 'Belts, belts, belts, an' that's one for you!'
      An' it was 'Belts, belts, belts, an' that's done for you!'
      O buckle an' tongue
      Was the song that we sung
      From Harrison's down to the Park!

There was a row in Silver Street – the regiments was out.
They called us 'Delhi Rebels,' an' we answered 'Threes about!'
That drew them like a hornets' nest – we met them good an'
   large,
The English at the double an' the Irish at the charge.
      Then it was: – 'Belts, &c.'

There was a row in Silver Street – an' I was in it too;
We passed the time o' day, an' then the belts went whirraru!
I misremember what occurred, but, subsequint the storm,
A *Freeman's Journal Supplemint* was all *my* uniform.
      O it was: – 'Belts, &c.'

There was a row in Silver Street – they sent the Polis there,
The English were too drunk to know, the Irish didn't care;
But when they grew impertinint we simultaneous rose,
Till half o' them was Liffey mud an' half was tatthered clo'es.
      For it was: – 'Belts, &c.'

There was a row in Silver Street – it might ha' raged till now,
But some one drew his side-arm clear, an' nobody knew how;
'Twas Hogan took the point an' dropped; we saw the red blood run:
An' so we all was murderers that started out in fun.
    While it was: 'Belts, &c.'

There was a row in Silver Street – but that put down the shine,
Wid each man whisperin' to his next: – "'Twas never work o' mine!'
We went away like beaten dogs, an' down the street we bore him,
The poor dumb corpse that couldn't tell the bhoys were sorry for him.
    When it was: – 'Belts, &c.'

There was a row in Silver Street – it isn't over yet,
For half of us are under guard wid punishments to get;
'Tis all a merricle to me as in the Clink I lie:
There was a row in Silver Street – begod, I wonder why!
    But it was: – 'Belts, belts, belts, an' that's one for you!'
    An' it was 'Belts, belts, belts, an' that's done for you!'
    O buckle an' tongue
    Was the song that we sung
    From Harrison's down to the Park!

MANDALAY

By the old Moulmein Pagoda, lookin' lazy at the sea,
There's a Burma girl a-settin', and I know she thinks o' me;
For the wind is in the palm-trees, and the temple-bells they say:
'Come you back, you British soldier; come you back to Mandalay!'
    Come you back to Mandalay,
    Where the old Flotilla lay:
    Can't you 'ear their paddles chunkin' from Rangoon to
        Mandalay?
    On the road to Mandalay,
    Where the flyin'-fishes play,
    An' the dawn comes up like thunder outer China 'crost the Bay!

'Er petticoat was yaller an' 'er little cap was green,
An' 'er name was Supi-yaw-lat – jes' the same as Theebaw's Queen,
An' I seed her first a-smokin' of a whackin' white cheroot,
An' a-wastin' Christian kisses on an 'eathen idol's foot:
    Bloomin' idol made o' mud –
    Wot they called the Great Gawd Budd –
    Plucky lot she cared for idols when I kissed 'er where she stud!
    On the road to Mandalay . . .

When the mist was on the rice-fields an' the sun was droppin' slow,
She'd git 'er little banjo an' she'd sing '*Kulla-lo-lo!*'
With 'er arm upon my shoulder an' 'er cheek agin my cheek
We useter watch the steamers an' the *hathis* pilin' teak.
    Elephints a-pilin' teak
    In the sludgy, squdgy creek,
    Where the silence 'ung that 'eavy you was 'arf afraid to speak!
    On the road to Mandalay . . .

But that's all shove be'ind me – long ago an' fur away,
An' there ain't no 'buses runnin' from the Bank to Mandalay;
An' I'm learnin' 'ere in London what the ten-year soldier tells:
'If you've 'eard the East a-callin', you won't never 'eed naught else.'
    No! you won't 'eed nothin' else
    But them spicy garlic smells,
    An' the sunshine an' the palm-trees an' the tinkly temple-bells;
    On the road to Mandalay . . .

I am sick o' wastin' leather on these gritty pavin'-stones,
An' the blasted English drizzle wakes the fever in my bones;
Tho' I walks with fifty 'ousemaids outer Chelsea to the Strand,
An' they talks a lot o' lovin', but wot do they understand?
    Beefy face an' grubby 'and –
    Law! wot do they understand?
    I've a neater, sweeter maiden in a cleaner, greener land!
    On the road to Mandalay . . .

Ship me somewheres east of Suez where the best is like the worst,
Where there aren't no Ten Commandments an' a man can raise a
  thirst;
For the temple-bells are callin', an' it's there that I would be –
By the old Moulmein Pagoda, looking lazy at the sea;
    On the road to Mandalay,
    Where the old Flotilla lay,
    With our sick beneath the awnings when we went to Manda-
      lay!
    O the road to Mandalay,
    Where the flyin'-fishes play,
    An' the dawn comes up like thunder outer China 'crost the Bay!

TROOPIN'

(Old English Army in the East)

Troopin', troopin', troopin' to the sea:
'Ere's September come again – the six-year men are free.
O leave the dead be'ind us, for they cannot come away
To where the ship's a-coalin' up that takes us 'ome to-day.
    We're goin' 'ome, we're goin' 'ome,
      Our ship is *at* the shore,
    An' you must pack your 'aversack,
      For we won't come back no more.
    Ho, don't you grieve for me,
      My lovely Mary-Ann!
    For I'll marry you yit on a fourp'ny bit
      As a time-expired man.

The *Malabar*'s in 'arbour with the *Jumner* at 'er tail,
An' the time-expired's waitin' of 'is orders for to sail.
Ho! the weary waitin' when on Khyber 'ills we lay,
But the time-expired's waitin' of 'is orders 'ome to-day.

They'll turn us out at Portsmouth wharf in cold an' wet an' rain,
All wearin' Injian cotton kit, but we will not complain.
They'll kill us of pneumonia – for that's their little way –
But damn the chills and fever, men, we're goin' 'ome to-day!

Troopin', troopin', winter's round again!
See the new draf's pourin' in for the old campaign;
Ho, you poor recruities, but you've got to earn your pay –
What's the last from Lunnon, lads? We're goin' there to-day.

Troopin', troopin', give another cheer –
'Ere's to English women an' a quart of English beer.
The Colonel an' the Regiment an' all who've got to stay,
Gawd's Mercy strike 'em gentle! Whoop! we're goin' 'ome
today.

We're goin' 'ome, we're goin' 'ome,
Our ship is *at* the shore,
An' you must pack your 'aversack,
For we won't come back no more.
Ho, don't you grieve for me,
My lovely Mary-Ann!
For I'll marry you yit on a fourp'ny bit
As a time-expired man.

FORD O' KABUL RIVER

Kabul town's by Kabul river –
  Blow the trumpet, draw the sword –
There I lef' my mate for ever,
  Wet an' drippin' by the ford.
    Ford, ford, ford o' Kabul river,
      Ford o' Kabul river in the dark!
    There's the river up and brimmin', an' there's 'arf a squadron swimmin'
      'Cross the ford o' Kabul river in the dark.

Kabul town's a blasted place –
  Blow the trumpet, draw the sword –
'Strewth I shan't forget 'is face
  Wet an' drippin' by the ford!
    Ford, ford, ford o' Kabul river,
      Ford o' Kabul river in the dark!
    Keep the crossing-stakes beside you, an' they will surely guide you
      'Cross the ford o' Kabul river in the dark.

Kabul town is sun and dust –
  Blow the trumpet, draw the sword –
I'd ha' sooner drownded fust
  'Stead of 'im beside the ford.
    Ford, ford, ford o' Kabul river,
      Ford o' Kabul river in the dark!
    You can 'ear the 'orses threshin'; you can 'ear the men a-splashin',
      'Cross the ford o' Kabul river in the dark.

Kabul town was ours to take –
  Blow the trumpet, draw the sword –
I'd ha' left it for 'is sake –
  'Im that left me by the ford.
    Ford, ford, ford o' Kabul river,
      Ford o' Kabul river in the dark!
    It's none so bloomin' dry there; ain't you never comin' nigh
        there,
      'Cross the ford o' Kabul river in the dark?

Kabul town'll go to hell –
  Blow the trumpet, draw the sword –
'Fore I see him 'live an' well –
  'Im the best beside the ford.
    Ford, ford, ford o' Kabul river,
      Ford o' Kabul river in the dark!
    Gawd 'elp 'em if they blunder, for their boots'll pull 'em under,
      By the ford o' Kabul river in the dark.

Turn your 'orse from Kabul town –
  Blow the trumpet, draw the sword –
'Im an' 'arf my troop is down,
  Down and drownded by the ford.
    Ford, ford, ford o' Kabul river,
      Ford o' Kabul river in the dark!
    There's the river low an' fallin', but it ain't no use a-callin'
      'Cross the ford o' Kabul river in the dark!

GENTLEMEN-RANKERS

To the legion of the lost ones, to the cohort of the damned,
  To my brethren in their sorrow overseas,
Sings a gentleman of England cleanly bred, machinely crammed,
  And a trooper of the Empress, if you please.
Yes, a trooper of the forces who has run his own six horses,
  And faith he went the pace and went it blind,
And the world was more than kin while he held the ready tin,
  But to-day the Sergeant's something less than kind.
    We're poor little lambs who've lost our way,
      Baa! Baa! Baa!
    We're little black sheep who've gone astray,
      Baa–aa–aa!
    Gentlemen-rankers out on the spree,
    Damned from here to Eternity,
    God ha' mercy on such as we,
      Baa! Yah! Bah!

Oh, it's sweet to sweat through stables, sweet to empty kitchen slops,
  And it's sweet to hear the tales the troopers tell,
To dance with blowzy housemaids at the regimental hops
  And thrash the cad who says you waltz too well.
Yes, it makes you cock-a-hoop to be 'Rider' to your troop,
  And branded with a blasted worsted spur,
When you envy, O how keenly, one poor Tommy living cleanly
  Who blacks your boots and sometimes calls you 'Sir'.

If the home we never write to, and the oaths we never keep,
  And all we know most distant and most dear,
Across the snoring barrack-room return to break our sleep,
  Can you blame us if we soak ourselves in beer?

When the drunken comrade mutters and the great guard-lantern
gutters
And the horror of our fall is written plain,
Every secret, self-revealing on the aching whitewashed ceiling,
Do you wonder that we drug ourselves from pain?

We have done with Hope and Honour, we are lost to Love and
Truth,
We are dropping down the ladder rung by rung,
And the measure of our torment is the measure of our youth.
God help us, for we knew the worst too young!
Our shame is clean repentance for the crime that brought the sent-
ence,
Our pride it is to know no spur of pride,
And the Curse of Reuben holds us till an alien turf enfolds us
And we die, and none can tell Them where we died.
We're poor little lambs who've lost our way,
Baa! Baa! Baa!
We're little black sheep who've gone astray,
Baa–aa–aa!
Gentlemen-rankers out on the spree,
Damned from here to Eternity,
God ha' mercy on such as we,
Baa! Yah! Bah!

'BACK TO THE ARMY AGAIN'

I'm 'ere in a ticky ulster an' a broken billycock 'at,
A-layin' on to the sergeant I don't know a gun from a bat;
My shirt's doin' duty for jacket, my sock's stickin' out o' my boots,
An' I'm learnin' the damned old goose-step along o' the new recruits!

Back to the Army again, sergeant,
 Back to the Army again.
Don't look so 'ard, for I 'aven't no card,
 I'm back to the Army again!

I done my six years' service. 'Er Majesty sez: 'Good day –
You'll please to come when you're rung for, an' 'ere's your 'ole
 back-pay;
An' fourpence a day for baccy – an' bloomin' gen'rous, too;
An' now you can make your fortune – the same as your orf'cers do.'

Back to the Army again, sergeant,
 Back to the Army again.
'Ow did I learn to do right-about-turn?
 I'm back to the Army again!

A man o' four-an'-twenty that 'asn't learned of a trade –
Beside 'Reserve' agin' him – 'e'd better be never made.
I tried my luck for a quarter, an' that was enough for me,
An' I thought of 'Er Majesty's barricks, an' I thought I'd go an' see.

Back to the Army again, sergeant,
 Back to the Army again.
'Tisn't my fault if I dress when I 'alt –
 I'm back to the Army again!

The sergeant arst no questions, but 'e winked the other eye,
'E sez to me, ''Shun!' an' I shunted, the same as in days gone by;
For 'e saw the set o' my shoulders, an' I couldn't 'elp 'oldin' straight
When me an' the other rookies come under the barrick-gate.

Back to the Army again, sergeant,
Back to the Army again.
'Oo would ha' thought I could carry an' port?[1]
I'm back to the Army again!

I took my bath, an' I wallered – for, Gawd, I needed it so!
I smelt the smell o' the barricks, I 'eard the bugles go.
I 'eard the feet on the gravel – the feet o' the men what drill –
An' I sez to my flutterin' 'eart-strings, I sez to 'em, 'Peace, be still!'

Back to the Army again, sergeant,
Back to the Army again.
'Oo said I knew when the troopship was due?
I'm back to the Army again!

I carried my slops to the tailor; I sez to 'im, 'None o' your lip!
You tight 'em over the shoulders, an' loose 'em over the 'ip,
For the set o' the tunic's 'orrid.' An' 'e sez to me, 'Strike me dead,
But I thought you was used to the business!' an' so 'e done what I said.

Back to the Army again, sergeant,
Back to the Army again.
Rather too free with my fancies? Wot – me?
I'm back to the Army again!

[1] Carry and port his rifle.

Next week I'll 'ave 'em fitted; I'll buy me a swagger-cane;
They'll let me free o' the barricks to walk on the Hoe again,
In the name o' William Parsons, that used to be Edward Clay,
An' – any pore beggar that wants it can draw my fourpence a day!

Back to the Army again, sergeant,
  Back to the Army again.
Out o' the cold an' the rain, sergeant,
  Out o' the cold an' the rain.
                    'Oo's there?

A man that's too good to be lost you,
  A man that is 'andled an' made –
A man that will pay what 'e cost you
  In learnin' the others their trade – parade!
You're droppin' the pick o' the Army
  Because you don't 'elp 'em remain,
But drives 'em to cheat to get out o' the street
  An' back to the Army again!

'BIRDS OF PREY' MARCH
(Troops for Foreign Service)

March! The mud is cakin' good about our trousies.
  Front! – eyes front, an' watch the Colour-casin's drip.
Front! The faces of the women in the 'ouses
  Ain't the kind o' things to take aboard the ship.

Cheer! An' we'll never march to victory.
Cheer! An' we'll never live to 'ear the cannon roar!
    The Large Birds o' Prey
    They will carry us away,
An' you'll never see your soldiers any more!

Wheel! Oh, keep your touch; we're goin' round a corner.
  Time! – mark time, an' let the men be'ind us close.
Lord! The transport's full, an' 'alf our lot not on 'er –
  Cheer, Oh, cheer! We're going off where no one knows.

March! The Devil's none so black as 'e is painted!
  Cheer! We'll 'ave some fun before we're put away.
'Alt an' 'and 'er out – a woman's gone and fainted!
  Cheer! Get on! – Gawd 'elp the married men to-day!

Hoi! Come up, you 'ungry beggars, to yer sorrow.
  ('Ear them say they want their tea, an' want it quick!)
You won't have no mind for slingers,[1] not to-morrow –
  No; you'll put the 'tween-decks stove out, bein' sick!

'Alt! The married kit 'as all to go before us!
  'Course it's blocked the bloomin' gangway up again!

[1] Bread soaked in tea.

Cheer, Oh, cheer the 'Orse Guards watchin' tender o'er us,
  Keepin' us since eight this mornin' in the rain!

Stuck in 'eavy marchin'-order, sopped and wringin' –
  Sick, before our time to watch 'er 'eave an' fall,
'Ere's your 'appy 'ome at last, an' stop your singin'.
  'Alt! Fall in along the troop-deck! Silence all!

Cheer! For we'll never live to see no bloomin' victory!
Cheer! An' we'll never live to 'ear the cannon roar!
    (*One cheer more!*)
      The jackal an' the kite
      'Ave an 'ealthy appetite,
An' you'll never see your soldiers any more! ('Ip! Urroar!)
      The eagle an' the crow
      They are waitin' ever so,
An' you'll never see your soldiers any more! ('Ip! Urroar!)
      Yes, the Large Birds o' Prey
      They will carry us away,
An' you'll never see your soldiers any more!

'SOLDIER AN' SAILOR TOO'

(The Royal Regiment of Marines)

As I was spittin' into the Ditch aboard o' the *Crocodile*,
I seed a man on a man-o'-war got up in the Reg'lars' style.
'E was scrapin' the paint from off of 'er plates, an' I sez to 'im, "'Oo
are you?'
Sez 'e, 'I'm a Jolly – 'Er Majesty's Jolly – soldier an' sailor too!'
Now 'is work begins by Gawd knows when, and 'is work is never
through;
'E isn't one o' the reg'lar Line, nor 'e isn't one of the crew.
'E's a kind of a giddy harumfrodite – soldier an' sailor too!

An', after, I met 'im all over the world, a-doin' all kinds of things,
Like landin' 'isself with a Gatlin' gun to talk to them 'eathen kings;
'E sleeps in an 'ammick instead of a cot, an' 'e drills with the deck on
a slew,
An' 'e sweats like a Jolly – 'Er Majesty's Jolly – soldier an' sailor
too!
For there isn't a job on the top o' the earth the beggar don't know,
nor do –
You can leave 'im at night on a bald man's 'ead, to paddle 'is own
canoe –
'E's a sort of a bloomin' cosmopolouse – soldier an' sailor too.

We've fought 'em in trooper, we've fought 'em in dock, and drunk
with 'em in betweens,
When they called us the seasick scull'ry-maids, an' we called 'em the
Ass-Marines;
But, when we was down for a double fatigue, from Woolwich to
Bernardmyo,

We sent for the Jollies – 'Er Majesty's Jollies – soldier an' sailor too!
They think for 'emselves, an' they steal for 'emselves, and they never ask what's to do,
But they're camped an' fed an' they're up an' fed before our bugle's blew.
Ho! they ain't no limpin' procrastitutes – soldier an' sailor too.

You may say we are fond of an 'arness-cut, or 'ootin' in barrick-yards,
Or startin' a Board School mutiny along o' the Onion Guards;[1]
But once in a while we can finish in style for the ends of the earth to view,
The same as the Jollies – 'Er Majesty's Jollies – soldier an' sailor too!
They come of our lot, they was brothers to us; they was beggars we'd met an' knew;
Yes, barrin' an inch in the chest an' the arm, they was doubles o' me an' you;
For they weren't no special chrysanthemums — soldier an' sailor too!

To take your chance in the thick of a rush, with firing all about,
Is nothing so bad when you've cover to 'and, an' leave an' likin' to shout;
But to stand an' be still to the *Birken'ead* drill[2] is a damn tough bullet to chew,
An' they done it, the Jollies – 'Er Majesty's Jollies – soldier an' sailor too!
Their work was done when it 'adn't begun; they was younger nor me an' you;

[1] Long ago, a battalion of the Guards was sent to Bermuda as a punishment for riotous conduct in barracks.

[2] In 1852 the *Birkenhead* transport was sunk off Simon's Bay. The Marines aboard her went down as drawn up on her deck.

Their choice it was plain between drownin' in 'eaps an' bein' mopped by the screw,
So they stood an' was still to the *Birken'ead* drill, soldier an' sailor too!

We're most of us liars, we're 'arf of us thieves, an' the rest are as rank as can be,
But once in a while we can finish in style (which I 'ope it won't 'appen to me).
But it makes you think better o' you an' your friends, an' the work you may 'ave to do,
When you think o' the sinkin' *Victorier*'s[1] Jollies – soldier an' sailor too!
Now there isn't no room for to say ye don't know – they 'ave proved it plain and true –
That, whether it's Widow, or whether it's ship, Victorier's work is to do,
An' they done it, the Jollies – 'Er Majesty's Jollies – soldier an' sailor too!

[1] Admiral Tryon's flagship, sunk in collision in 1893.

'THE MEN THAT FOUGHT AT MINDEN'

(In the Lodge of Instruction)

The men that fought at Minden, they was rookies in their time –
  So was them that fought at Waterloo!
All the 'ole command, yuss, from Minden to Maiwand,
  They was once dam' sweeps like you!

Then do not be discouraged, 'Eaven is your 'elper,
  We'll learn you not to forget;
An' you mustn't swear an' curse, or you'll only catch it worse,
  For we'll make you soldiers yet!

The men that fought at Minden, they 'ad stocks beneath their chins,
  Six inch 'igh an' more;
But fatigue it was their pride, and they *would* not be denied
  To clean the cook-'ouse floor.

The men that fought at Minden, they had anarchistic bombs
  Served to 'em by name of 'and-grenades;
But they got it in the eye (same as you will by-an'-by)
  When they clubbed their field-parades.

The men that fought at Minden, they 'ad buttons up an' down,
  Two-an'-twenty dozen of 'em told;
But they didn't grouse an' shirk at an hour's extry work,
  They kept 'em bright as gold.

The men that fought at Minden, they was armed with musketoons,
  Also, they was drilled by 'alberdiers.
I don't know what they were, but the sergeants took good care
  They washed be'ind their ears.

The men that fought at Minden, they 'ad ever cash in 'and
Which they did not bank nor save,
But spent it gay an' free on their betters – such as me –
For the good advice I gave.

The men that fought at Minden, they was civil – yuss, they was –
Never didn't talk o' rights an' wrongs,
But they got it with the toe (same as you will get it – so!) –
For interrupting songs.

The men that fought at Minden, they was several other things
Which I don't remember clear;
But *that's* the reason why, now the six-year men are dry,
The rooks will stand the beer!

Then do not be discouraged, 'Eaven is your 'elper,
We'll learn you not to forget;
An' you mustn't swear an' curse, or you'll only catch it worse,
An' we'll make you soldiers yet!

Soldiers yet, if you've got it in you –
All for the sake of the Core;
Soldiers yet, if we 'ave to skin you –
Run an' get the beer, Johnny Raw – Johnny Raw!
Ho! run and get the beer, Johnny Raw!

CHOLERA CAMP
(Infantry in India)

We've got the cholerer in camp – it's worse than forty fights;
We're dyin' in the wilderness the same as Isrulites.
It's before us, an' be'ind us, an' we cannot get away,
An' the doctor's just reported we've ten more to-day!

Oh, strike your camp an' go, the Bugle's callin',
The Rains are fallin' –
The dead are bushed an' stoned to keep 'em safe below.
The Band's a-doin' all she knows to cheer us;
The Chaplain's gone and prayed to Gawd to 'ear us –
To 'ear us –
O Lord, for it's a-killin' of us so!

Since August, when it started, it's been stickin' to our tail,
Though they've 'ad us out by marches an' they've 'ad us back by rail;
But it runs as fast as troop trains, and we cannot get away,
An' the sick-list to the Colonel makes ten more to-day.

There ain't no fun in women nor there ain't no bite to drink;
It's much too wet for shootin'; we can only march and think;
An' at evenin', down the *nullahs*, we can 'ear the jackals say,
'Get up, you rotten beggars, you've ten more to-day!'

'Twould make a monkey cough to see our way o' doin' things –
Lieutenants takin' companies an' Captains takin' wings,
An' Lances actin' Sergeants – eight file to obey –
For we've lots o' quick promotion on ten deaths a day!

Our Colonel's white an' twitterly – 'e gets no sleep nor food,
But mucks about in 'orspital where nothing does no good.
'E sends us 'eaps o' comforts, all bought from 'is pay –
But there aren't much comfort 'andy on ten deaths a day.

Our Chaplain's got a banjo, an' a skinny mule 'e rides,
An' the stuff he says an' sings us, Lord, it makes us split our sides!
With 'is black coat-tails a-bobbin' to *Ta-ra-ra Boom-der-ay*!
'E's the proper kind o' *padre* for ten deaths a day.

An' Father Victor 'elps 'im with our Roman Catholicks –
He knows an 'eap of Irish songs an' rummy conjurin'-tricks;
An' the two they works together when it comes to play or pray.
So we keep the ball a-rollin' on ten deaths a day.

We've got the cholerer in camp – we've got it 'ot an' sweet.
It ain't no Christmas dinner, but it's 'elped an' we must eat.
We've gone beyond the funkin', 'cause we've found it doesn't pay,
An' we're rockin' round the Districk on ten deaths a day!

Then strike your camp an' go, the Rains are fallin',
The Bugle's callin!
The dead are bushed an' stoned to keep 'em safe below!
An' them that do not like it they can lump it,
An' them that cannot stand it they can jump it;
We've got to die somewhere – some way – some'ow –
We might as well begin to do it now!
Then, Number One, let down the tent-pole slow,
Knock out the pegs an' 'old the corners – so!
Fold in the flies, furl up the ropes, an' stow!
Oh, strike – oh, strike your camp an' go!
(*Gawd 'elp us!*)

THE LADIES

I've taken my fun where I've found it;
  I've rogued an' I've ranged in my time;
I've 'ad my pickin' o' sweethearts,
  An' four o' the lot was prime.
One was an 'arf-caste widow,
  One was a woman at Prome,
One was the wife of a *jemadar-sais*,[1]
  An' one is a girl at 'ome.

Now I aren't no 'and with the ladies,
  For takin' 'em all along,
You never can say till you've tried 'em,
  An' then you are like to be wrong.
There's times when you'll think that you mightn't,
  There's times when you'll know that you might;
But the things you will learn from the Yellow an' Brown,
  They'll 'elp you a lot with the White!

I was a young un at 'Oogli,
  Shy as a girl to begin;
Aggie de Castrer she made me,
  An' Aggie was clever as sin;
Older than me, but my first un –
  More like a mother she were –
Showed me the way to promotion an' pay,
  An' I learned about women from 'er!

Then I was ordered to Burma,
  Actin' in charge o' Bazar,

[1] Head-groom.

An' I got me a tiddy live 'eathen
  Through buyin' supplies off 'er pa.
Funny an' yellow an' faithful –
  Doll in a teacup she were –
But we lived on the square, like a true-married pair,
  An' I learned about women from 'er!

Then we was shifted to Neemuch
  (Or I might ha' been keepin' 'er now),
An' I took with a shiny she-devil,
  The wife of a nigger at Mhow;
'Taught me the gipsy-folks' *bolee*;[1]
  Kind o' volcano she were,
For she knifed me one night 'cause I wished she was white,
  And I learned about women from 'er!

Then I come 'ome in a trooper,
  'Long of a kid o' sixteen –
'Girl from a convent at Meerut,
  The straightest I ever 'ave seen.
Love at first sight was 'er trouble,
  She didn't know what it were;
An' I wouldn't do such, 'cause I liked 'er too much,
  But – I learned about women from 'er!

I've taken my fun where I've found it,
  An' now I must pay for my fun,
For the more you 'ave known o' the others
  The less will you settle to one;
An' the end of it's sittin' and thinkin',
  An' dreamin' Hell-fires to see;
So be warned by my lot (which I know you will not),
  An' learn about women from me!

[1] Slang.

What did the Colonel's Lady think?
  Nobody never knew.
Somebody asked the Sergeant's Wife,
  An' *she told 'em true!*
When you get to a man in the case,
  They're like as a row of pins –
For the Colonel's Lady an' Judy O'Grady
  Are sisters under their skins!

THE MOTHER-LODGE

There was Rundle, Station Master,
An' Beazeley of the Rail,
An' 'Ackman, Commissariat,
  An' Donkin o' the Jail;
An' Blake, Conductor-Sergeant,
  Our Master twice was 'e,
With 'im that kept the Europe-shop,
  Old Framjee Eduljee.

Outside – 'Sergeant! Sir! Salute! Salaam!'
Inside – 'Brother,' an' it doesn't do no 'arm.
We met upon the Level an' we parted on the Square,
An' I was Junior Deacon in my Mother-Lodge out there!

We'd Bola Nath, Accountant,
  An' Saul the Aden Jew,
An' Din Mohammed, draughtsman
  Of the Survey Office too;
There was Babu Chuckerbutty,
  An' Amir Singh the Sikh,
An' Castro from the fittin'-sheds,
  The Roman Catholick!

We 'adn't good regalia,
  An' our Lodge was old an' bare,
But we knew the Ancient Landmarks,
  An' we kep' 'em to a hair;
An' lookin' on it backwards
  It often strikes me thus,

There ain't such things as infidels,
  Excep', per'aps, it's us.

For monthly, after Labour,
  We'd all sit down and smoke
(We dursn't give no banquets,
  Lest a Brother's caste were broke),
An' man on man got talkin'
  Religion an' the rest,
An' every man comparin'
  Of the God 'e knew the best.

So man on man got talkin',
  An' not a Brother stirred
Till mornin' waked the parrots
  An' that dam' brain-fever-bird;
We'd say 'twas 'ighly curious,
  An' we'd all ride 'ome to bed,
With Mo'ammed, God, an' Shiva
  Changin' pickets in our 'ead.

Full oft on Guv'ment service
  This rovin' foot 'ath pressed,
An' bore fraternal greetin's
  To the Lodges east an' west,
Accordin' as commanded,
  From Kohat to Singapore,
But I wish that I might see them
  In my Mother-Lodge once more!

I wish that I might see them,
  My Brethren black an' brown,

With the trichies smellin' pleasant
An' the *hog-darn*[1] passin' down;
An' the old khansamah[2] snorin'
On the bottle-khana[3] floor,
Like a Master in good standing
With my Mother-Lodge once more.

Outside – 'Sergeant! Sir! Salute! Salaam!'
Inside – 'Brother,' an' it doesn't do no 'arm.
We met upon the Level an' we parted on the Square,
An' I was Junior Deacon in my Mother-Lodge out there!

[1] Cigar-lighter. [2] Butler. [3] Pantry.

FOLLOW ME 'OME

There was no one like 'im, 'Orse or Foot,
  Nor any o' the Guns I knew;
An' because it was so, why, o' course 'e went an' died,
    Which is just what the best men do.

  So it's knock out your pipes an' follow me!
  An' it's finish up your swipes an' follow me!
    Oh, 'ark to the big drum callin',
      Follow me – follow me 'ome!

  'Is mare she neighs the 'ole day long,
    She paws the 'ole night through,
An' she won't take 'er feed 'cause o' waitin' for 'is step,
    Which is just what a beast would do.

  'Is girl she goes with a bombardier
    Before 'er month is through;
An' the banns are up in church, for she's got the beggar hooked,
    Which is just what a girl would do.

  We fought 'bout a dog – last week it were –
    No more than a round or two;
But I strook 'im cruel 'ard, an' I wish I 'adn't now,
    Which is just what a man can't do.

  'E was all that I 'ad in the way of a friend,
    An' I've 'ad to find one new;
But I'd give my pay an' stripe for to get the beggar back,
    Which it's just too late to do!

So it's knock out your pipes an' follow me!
An' it's finish up your swipes an' follow me!
Oh, 'ark to the fifes a-crawlin'!
Follow me – follow me 'ome!

Take 'im away! 'E's gone where the best men go.
Take 'im away! An' the gun-wheels turnin' slow.
Take 'im away! There's more from the place 'e come.
Take 'im away, with the limber an' the drum.

For it's 'Three rounds blank' an' follow me,
An' it's 'Thirteen rank' an' follow me;
Oh, passin' the love o' women,
Follow me – follow me 'ome!

THE SERGEANT'S WEDDIN'

'E was warned agin 'er –
 That's what made 'im look;
She was warned agin' 'im –
 That is why she took.
'Wouldn't 'ear no reason,
 'Went an' done it blind;
We know all about 'em,
 They've got all to find!

Cheer for the Sergeant's weddin' –
 Give 'em one cheer more!
Grey gun-'orses in the lando,
 An' a rogue is married to, etc.

What's the use o' tellin'
 'Arf the lot she's been?
'E's a bloomin' robber,
 An' 'e keeps canteen.
'Ow did 'e get 'is buggy?
 Gawd, you needn't ask!
'Made 'is forty gallon
 Out of every cask!

Watch 'im, with 'is 'air cut,
 Count us filin' by –
Won't the Colonel praise 'is
 Pop–u–lar–i–ty!
We 'ave scores to settle –
 Scores for more than beer;

She's the girl to pay 'em –
  That is why we're 'ere!

See the Chaplain thinkin'?
  See the women smile?
Twig the married winkin'
  As they take the aisle?
Keep your side-arms quiet,
  Dressin' by the Band.
Ho! You 'oly beggars,
  Cough be'ind your 'and!

Now it's done an' over,
  'Ear the organ squeak,
"*Voice that breathed o'er Eden*' –
  Ain't she got the cheek!
White an' laylock ribbons,
  'Think yourself so fine!
I'd pray Gawd to take yer
  'Fore I made yer mine!

Escort to the kerridge,
  Wish 'im luck, the brute!
Chuck the slippers after –
  (Pity 'tain't a boot!)
Bowin' like a lady,
  Blushin' like a lad –
'Oo would say to see 'em
  Both is rotten bad?

Cheer for the Sergeant's weddin' –
  Give 'em one cheer more!
Grey gun-'orses in the lando,
  An' a rogue is married to, etc.

THE 'EATHEN

The 'eathen in 'is blindness bows down to wood an' stone;
'E don't obey no orders unless they is 'is own;
'E keeps 'is side-arms awful: 'e leaves 'em all about,
An' then comes up the Regiment an' pokes the 'eathen out.

All along o' dirtiness, all along o' mess,
All along o' doin' things rather-more-or-less,
All along of abby-nay,[1] *kul,*[2] *an' hazar-ho,*[3]
Mind you keep your rifle an' yourself jus' so!

The young recruit is 'aughty – 'e draf's from Gawd knows where;
They bid 'im show 'is stockin's an' lay 'is mattress square;
'E calls it bloomin' nonsense – 'e doesn't know, no more –
An' then up comes 'is Company an' kicks 'im round the floor!

The young recruit is 'ammered – 'e takes it very hard;
'E 'angs 'is 'ead an' mutters – 'e sulks about the yard;
'E talks o' 'cruel tyrants' which 'e'll swing for by-an'-by,
An' the others 'ears an' mocks 'im, an' the boy goes orf to cry.

The young recruit is silly – 'e thinks o' suicide.
'E's lost 'is gutter-devil; 'e 'asn't got 'is pride;
But day by day they kicks 'im, which 'elps 'im on a bit,
Till 'e finds 'isself one mornin' with a full an' proper kit.

Gettin' clear o' dirtiness, gettin' done with mess,
Gettin' shut o' doin' things rather-more-or-less;
Not so fond of abby-nay, kul, nor hazar-ho,
Learns to keep 'is rifle an' 'isself jus' so!

[1] Not now. [2] To-morrow. [3] Wait a bit.

The young recruit is 'appy – 'e throws a chest to suit;
You see 'im grow mustaches; you 'ear 'im slap 'is boot.
'E learns to drop the 'bloodies' from every word 'e slings,
An' 'e shows an 'ealthy brisket when 'e strips for bars an' rings.

The cruel-tyrant-sergeants they watch 'im 'arf a year;
They watch 'im with 'is comrades, they watch 'im with 'is beer;
They watch 'im with the women at the regimental dance,
And the cruel-tyrant-sergeants send 'is name along for 'Lance'.

An' now 'e's 'arf o' nothin', an' all a private yet,
'Is room they up an' rags 'im to see what they will get.
They rags 'im low an' cunnin', each dirty trick they can,
But 'e learns to sweat 'is temper an' 'e learns to sweat 'is man.

An', last, a Colour-Sergeant, as such to be obeyed,
'E schools 'is men at cricket, 'e tells 'em on parade;
They sees 'im quick an' 'andy, uncommon set an' smart,
An' so 'e talks to orficers which 'ave the Core at 'eart.

'E learns to do 'is watchin' without it showin' plain;
'E learns to save a dummy, an' shove 'im straight again;
'E learns to check a ranker that's buyin' leave to shirk;
An' 'e learns to make men like 'im so they'll learn to like their work.

An' when it comes to marchin' he'll see their socks are right,
An' when it comes to action 'e shows 'em how to sight.
'E knows their ways of thinkin' and just what's in their mind;
'E knows when they are takin' on an' when they've fell be'ind.

'E knows each talkin' corp'ral that leads a squad astray;
'E feels 'is innards 'eavin', 'is bowels givin' way;
'E sees the blue-white faces all tryin' 'ard to grin,
An' 'e stands an' waits an' suffers till it's time to cap 'em in.

An' now the hugly bullets come peckin' through the dust,
An' no one wants to face 'em, but every beggar must;
So, like a man in irons, which isn't glad to go,
They moves 'em off by companies uncommon stiff an' slow.

Of all 'is five years' schoolin' they don't remember much
Excep' the not retreatin', the step an' keepin' touch.
It looks like teachin' wasted when they duck an' spread an' 'op –
But if 'e 'adn't learned 'em they'd be all about the shop.

An' now it's ''Oo goes backward?' an' now it's ''Oo comes on?'
And now it's 'Get the doolies,' an' now the Captain's gone;
An' now it's bloody murder, but all the while they 'ear
'Is voice, the same as barrick-drill, a-shepherdin' the rear.

'E's just as sick as they are, 'is 'eart is like to split,
But 'e works 'em, works 'em, works 'em till he feels 'em take the bit;
The rest is 'oldin' steady till the watchful bugles play,
An' 'e lifts 'em, lifts 'em, lifts 'em through the charge that wins the
day!

The 'eathen in 'is blindness bows down to wood an' stone;
'E don't obey no orders unless they is 'is own.
The 'eathen in 'is blindness must end where 'e began,
But the backbone of the Army is the Non-commissioned Man!

Keep away from dirtiness – keep away from mess,
Don't get into doin' things rather-more-or-less!
Let's ha' done with abby-nay, kul, and hazar-ho;
Mind you keep your rifle an' yourself jus' so!

'MARY, PITY WOMEN!'

You call yourself a man,
  For all you used to swear,
An' leave me, as you can,
  My certain shame to bear?
  I 'ear! You do not care –
You done the worst you know.
  I 'ate you, grinnin' there . . .
Ah, Gawd, I love you so!

Nice while it lasted, an' now it is over –
Tear out your 'eart an' good-bye to your lover!
What's the use o' grievin', when the mother that bore you
(Mary, pity women!) knew it all before you?

It aren't no false alarm,
  The finish to your fun;
You – you 'ave brung the 'arm,
  An' I'm the ruined one!
  An' now you'll off an' run
With some new fool in tow.
  Your 'eart? You 'aven't none . . .
Ah, Gawd, I love you so!

When a man is tired there is naught will bind 'im;
All 'e solemn promised 'e will shove be'ind 'im.
What's the good o' prayin' for The Wrath to strike 'im
(Mary, pity women!), when the rest are like 'im?

What 'ope for me or – it?
  What's left for us to do?

I've walked with men a bit,
But this – but this is you.
So 'elp me, Christ, it's true!
Where can I 'ide or go?
You coward through and through! . . .
Ah, Gawd, I love you so!

All the more you give 'em the less are they for givin' –
Love lies dead, an' you cannot kiss 'im livin'.
Down the road 'e led you there is no returnin'
(Mary, pity women!), but you're late in learnin'!

You'd like to treat me fair?
You can't, because we're pore?
We'd starve? What do I care!
We might, but *this* is shore!
I want the name – no more –
The name, an' lines to show,
An' not to be an 'ore . . .
Ah, Gawd, I love you so!

What's the good o' pleadin', when the mother that bore you
(Mary, pity women!) knew it all before you?
Sleep on 'is promises an' wake to your sorrow
(Mary, pity women!), for we sail to-morrow!

'FOR TO ADMIRE'

The Injian Ocean sets an' smiles
So sof', so bright, so bloomin' blue;
There aren't a wave for miles an' miles
Excep' the jiggle from the screw.
The ship is swep', the day is done,
The bugle's gone for smoke and play;
An' black ag'in the settin' sun
The Lascar sings, '*Hum deckty hai!*'[1]

For to admire an' for to see,
For to be'old this world so wide –
It never done no good to me,
But I can't drop it if I tried!

I see the sergeants pitchin' quoits,
I 'ear the women laugh an' talk,
I spy upon the quarter-deck
The orficers an' lydies walk.
I thinks about the things that was,
An' leans an' looks acrost the sea,
Till, spite of all the crowded ship,
There's no one lef' alive but me.

The things that was which I 'ave seen,
In barrick, camp, an' action too,
I tells them over by myself,
An' sometimes wonders if they're true;
For they was odd – most awful odd –
But all the same, now they are o'er,

[1] I'm looking out.

There must be 'eaps o' plenty such,
  An' if I wait I'll see some more.

Oh, I 'ave come upon the books,
  An' frequent broke a barrick-rule,
An' stood beside an' watched myself
  Be'avin' like a bloomin' fool.
I paid my price for findin' out,
  Nor never grutched the price I paid,
But sat in Clink without my boots,
  Admirin' 'ow the world was made.

Be'old a cloud upon the beam,
  An' 'umped above the sea appears
Old Aden, like a barrick-stove
  That no one's lit for years an' years.
I passed by that when I began,
  An' I go 'ome the road I came,
A time-expired soldier-man
  With six years' service to 'is name.

My girl she said, 'Oh, stay with me!'
  My mother 'eld me to 'er breast.
They've never written none, an' so
  They must 'ave gone with all the rest –
With all the rest which I 'ave seen
  An' found an' known an' met along.
I cannot say the things I feel,
  And so I sing my evenin' song:

For to admire an' for to see,
  For to be'old this world so wide –
It never done no good to me,
  But I can't drop it if I tried!

THE ABSENT-MINDED BEGGAR

When you've shouted 'Rule Britannia', when you've sung 'God save the Queen',
When you've finished killing Kruger with your mouth,
Will you kindly drop a shilling in my little tambourine
For a gentleman in khaki ordered South?
He's an absent-minded beggar, and his weaknesses are great –
But we and Paul[1] must take him as we find him –
He is out on active service, wiping something off a slate –
And he's left a lot of little things behind him!
Duke's son – cook's son – son of a hundred kings –
(Fifty thousand horse and foot going to Table Bay!)
Each of 'em doing his country's work
(and who's to look after their things?)
Pass the hat for your credit's sake,
and pay – pay – pay!

There are girls he married secret, asking no permission to,
For he knew he wouldn't get it if he did.
There is gas and coals and vittles, and the house-rent falling due,
And it's more than rather likely there's a kid.
There are girls he walked with casual. They'll be sorry now he's gone,
For an absent-minded beggar they will find him,
But it ain't the time for sermons with the winter coming on.
We must help the girl that Tommy's left behind him!
Cook's son – Duke's son – son of a belted Earl –
Son of a Lambeth publican – it's all the same to-day!
Each of 'em doing his country's work
(and who's to look after the girl?)

[1] i.e. Paul Kruger. (Ed.)

Pass the hat for your credit's sake,
and pay – pay – pay!

There are families by thousands, far too proud to beg or speak,
And they'll put their sticks and bedding up the spout,
And they'll live on half o' nothing, paid 'em punctual once a week,
'Cause the man that earns the wage is ordered out.
He's an absent-minded beggar, but he heard his country call,
And his reg'ment didn't need to send to find him!
He chucked his job and joined it – so the job before us all
Is to help the home that Tommy's left behind him!
Duke's job – cook's job – gardener, baronet, groom,
Mews or palace or paper-shop, there's someone gone away!
Each of 'em doing his country's work
(and who's to look after the room?)
Pass the hat for your credit's sake,
and pay – pay – pay!

Let us manage so as, later, we can look him in the face,
And tell him – what he'd very much prefer –
That, while he saved the Empire, his employer saved his place,
And his mates (that's you and me) looked out for *her*.
He's an absent-minded beggar and he may forget it all,
But we do not want his kiddies to remind him
That we sent 'em to the workhouse while their daddy hammered
Paul,
So we'll help the homes that Tommy left behind him!
Cook's home – Duke's home – home of a millionaire,
(Fifty thousand horse and foot going to Table Bay!)
Each of 'em doing his country's work
(and what have you got to spare?)
Pass the hat for your credit's sake,
and pay – pay – pay!

CHANT-PAGAN
(English Irregular, Discharged)

Me that 'ave been what I've been –
Me that 'ave gone where I've gone –
Me that 'ave seen what I've seen –
  'Ow can I ever take on
With awful old England again,
An' 'ouses both sides of the street,
And 'edges two sides of the lane,
And the parson an' gentry between,
An' touchin' my 'at when we meet –
  Me that 'ave been what I've been?

Me that 'ave watched 'arf a world
'Eave up all shiny with dew,
Kopje on kop to the sun,
An' as soon as the mist let 'em through
Our 'elios winkin' like fun –
Three sides of a ninety-mile square,
Over valleys as big as a shire –
'*Are ye there? Are ye there? Are ye there?*'
An' then the blind drum of our fire . . .
An' I'm rollin' 'is lawns for the Squire,
                Me!

Me that 'ave rode through the dark
Forty mile, often, on end,
Along the Ma'ollisberg Range,
With only the stars for my mark
An' only the night for my friend,

An' things runnin' off as you pass,
An' things jumpin' up in the grass,
An' the silence, the shine an' the size
Of the 'igh, unexpressible skies –
I am takin' some letters almost
As much as a mile to the post,
An' 'mind you come back with the change!'
Me!

Me that saw Barberton took
When we dropped through the clouds on their 'ead,
An' they 'ove the guns over and fled –
Me that was through Di'mond 'Ill,
An' Pieters an' Springs an' Belfast –
From Dundee to Vereeniging all –
Me that stuck out to the last
(An' five bloomin' bars on my chest) –
I am doin' my Sunday-school best,
By the 'elp of the Squire an' 'is wife
(Not to mention the 'ousemaid an' cook),
To come in an' 'ands up an' be still,
An' honestly work for my bread,
My livin' in that state of life
To which it shall please God to call
Me!

Me that 'ave followed my trade
In the place where the Lightnin's are made;
'Twixt the Rains and the Sun and the Moon –
Me that lay down an' got up
Three years with the sky for my roof –
That 'ave ridden my 'unger an' thirst
Six thousand raw mile on the hoof,

With the Vaal and the Orange for cup,
An' the Brandwater Basin for dish, –
Oh! it's 'ard to be'ave as they wish
(Too 'ard, an' a little too soon),
I'll 'ave to think over it first –
Me!

I will arise an' get 'ence –
I will trek South and make sure
If it's only my fancy or not
That the sunshine of England is pale,
And the breezes of England are stale,
An' there's somethin' gone small with the lot.
For *I* know of a sun an' a wind,
An' some plains and a mountain be'ind,
An' some graves by a barb-wire fence,
An' a Dutchman I've fought 'oo might give
Me a job were I ever inclined
To look in an' offsaddle an' live
Where there's neither a road nor a tree –
But only my Maker an' me,
And I think it will kill me or cure,
So I think I will go there an' see.
Me!

BOOTS
(Infantry Columns)

We're foot – slog – slog – slog – sloggin' over Africa –
Foot – foot – foot – foot – sloggin' over Africa –
(Boots – boots – boots – boots – movin' up and down again!)
        There's no discharge in the war!

Seven – six – eleven – five – nine-an'-twenty mile to-day –
Four – eleven – seventeen – thirty-two the day before –
(Boots – boots – boots – boots – movin' up and down again!)
        There's no discharge in the war!

Don't–don't–don't–don't–look at what's in front of you.
(Boots–boots–boots–boots–movin' up an' down again);
Men – men – men – men – men go mad with watchin' 'em,
        An' there's no discharge in the war!

Try – try – try – try – to think o' something different –
Oh – my – God – keep – me from goin' lunatic!
(Boots – boots – boots – boots – movin' up an' down again!)
        There's no discharge in the war!

Count – count – count – count – the bullets in the bandoliers.
If – your – eyes – drop – they will get atop o' you!
(Boots – boots – boots – boots – movin' up and down again) –
        There's no discharge in the war!

We – can – stick – out – 'unger, thirst, an' weariness,
But – not – not – not – not the chronic sight of 'em –
Boots – boots – boots – boots – movin' up an' down again,
        An' there's no discharge in the war!

'Tain't – so – bad – by – day because o' company,
But night – brings – long – strings – o' forty thousand million
Boots – boots – boots – boots – movin' up an' down again.
  There's no discharge in the war!

I – 'ave – marched – six – weeks in 'Ell an' certify
It – is – not – fire – devils, dark, or anything,
But boots – boots – boots – boots – movin' up an' down again,
  An' there's no discharge in the war!

THE MARRIED MAN
(Reservist of the Line)

The bachelor 'e fights for one
  As joyful as can be;
But the married man don't call it fun,
  Because 'e fights for three –
For 'Im an' 'Er an' It
  (An' Two an' One make Three)
'E wants to finish 'is little bit,
  An' 'e wants to go 'ome to 'is tea!

The bachelor pokes up 'is 'ead
  To see if you are gone;
But the married man lies down instead,
  An' waits till the sights come on,
For 'Im an' 'Er an' a hit
  (Direct or ricochee)
'E wants to finish 'is little bit,
  An' 'e wants to go 'ome to 'is tea.

The bachelor will miss you clear
  To fight another day;
But the married man, 'e says 'No fear!'
  'E wants you out of the way
Of 'Im an' 'Er an' It
  (An' 'is road to 'is farm or the sea),
'E wants to finish 'is little bit,
  An' 'e wants to go 'ome to 'is tea.

The bachelor 'e fights 'is fight
  An' stretches out an' snores;

But the married man sits up all night –
  For 'e don't like out-o'-doors.
'E'll strain an' listen an' peer
  An' give the first alarm –
For the sake o' the breathin' 'e's used to 'ear,
  An' the 'ead on the thick of 'is arm.

The bachelor may risk 'is 'ide
  To 'elp you when you're drowned;
But the married man will wait beside
  Till the ambulance comes round.
'E'll take your 'ome address
  An' all you've time to say,
Or if 'e sees there's 'ope, 'e'll press
  Your art'ry 'alf the day –

For 'Im an' 'Er an' It
  (An' One from Three leaves Two),
For 'e knows you wanted to finish your bit,
  An' 'e knows 'oo's wantin' you.
Yes, 'Im an' 'Er an' It
  (Our 'oly One in Three),
We're all of us anxious to finish our bit,
  An' we want to get 'ome to our tea!

Yes, It an' 'Er an' 'Im,
  Which often makes me think
The married man must sink or swim
  An' – 'e can't afford to sink!
Oh, 'Im an' It an' 'Er
  Since Adam an' Eve began!
So I'd rather fight with the bachel*er*
  An' be nursed by the married man!

LICHTENBERG
(New South Wales Contingent)

Smells are surer than sounds or sights
  To make your heart-strings crack –
They start those awful voices o' nights
  That whisper, 'Old man, come back!'
That must be why the big things pass
  And the little things remain,
Like the smell of the wattle by Lichtenberg,
  Riding in, in the rain.

There was some silly fire on the flank
  And the small wet drizzling down –
There were the sold-out shops and the bank
  And the wet, wide-open town;
And we were doing escort-duty
  To somebody's baggage-train,
And I smelt wattle by Lichtenberg –
  Riding in, in the rain.

It was all Australia to me –
  All I had found or missed:
Every face I was crazy to see,
  And every woman I'd kissed:
All that I shouldn't ha' done, God knows!
  (As He knows I'll do it again),
That smell of the wattle round Lichtenberg,
  Riding in, in the rain!

And I saw Sydney the same as ever,
  The picnics and brass-bands;

And my little homestead on Hunter River
  And my new vines joining hands.
It all came over me in one act
  Quick as a shot through the brain –
With the smell of the wattle round Lichtenberg,
  Riding in, in the rain.

I have forgotten a hundred fights,
  But one I shall not forget –
With the raindrops bunging up my sights
  And my eyes bunged up with wet;
And through the crack and the stink of the cordite,
  (Ah, Christ! My country again!)
The smell of the wattle by Lichtenberg,
  Riding in, in the rain!

HALF-BALLADE OF WATERVAL
(Non-commissioned Officers in Charge of Prisoners)

When by the labour of my 'ands
  I've 'elped to pack a transport tight
With prisoners for foreign lands,
  I ain't transported with delight.
  I know it's only just an' right,
    But yet it somehow sickens me,
For I 'ave learned at Waterval[1]
    The meanin' of captivity.

Be'ind the pegged barb-wire strands,
  Beneath the tall electric light,
We used to walk in bare-'ead bands,
  Explainin' 'ow we lost our fight;
  An' that is what they'll do to-night
    Upon the steamer out at sea,
If I 'ave learned at Waterval
    The meanin' of captivity.

They'll never know the shame that brands –
  Black shame no livin' down makes white –
The mockin' from the sentry-stands,
  The women's laugh, the gaoler's spite.
  We are too bloomin'-much polite,
    But that is 'ow I'd 'ave us be ...
Since I 'ave learned at Waterval
    The meanin' of captivity.

[1] Where the majority of English prisoners were kept by the Boers.

They'll get those draggin' days all right,
Spent as a foreigner commands,
An' 'orrors of the locked-up night,
With 'Ell's own thinkin' on their 'ands.
I'd give the gold o' twenty Rands
(If it was mine) to set 'em free,
For I 'ave learned at Waterval
The meanin' of captivity!

THE RETURN
(All Arms)

Peace is declared, an' I return
  To 'Ackneystadt, but not the same;
Things 'ave transpired which made me learn
  The size and meanin' of the game.
I did no more than others did,
  I don't know where the change began.
I started as a average kid,
  I finished as a thinkin' man.

If England was what England seems,
  An' not the England of our dreams,
But only putty, brass, an' paint,
  'Ow quick we'd drop 'er! But she ain't!

Before my gappin' mouth could speak
  I 'eard it in my comrade's tone.
I saw it on my neighbour's cheek
  Before I felt it flush my own.
An' last it come to me – not pride,
  Nor yet conceit, but on the 'ole
(If such a term may be applied),
  The makin's of a bloomin' soul.

Rivers at night that cluck an' jeer,
  Plains which the moonshine turns to sea,
Mountains which never let you near,
  An' stars to all eternity;
An' the quick-breathin' dark that fills
  The 'ollows of the wilderness,

When the wind worries through the 'ills –
   These may 'ave taught me more or less.

Towns without people, ten times took,
   An' ten times left an' burned at last;
An' starvin' dogs that come to look
   For owners when a column passed;
An' quiet, 'omesick talks between
   Men, met by night, you never knew
Until – 'is face – by shellfire seen –
   Once – an' struck off. *They* taught me too.

The day's lay-out – the mornin' sun
   Beneath your 'at-brim as you sight;
The dinner-'ush from noon till one,
   An' the full roar that lasts till night;
An' the pore dead that look so old
   An' was so young an hour ago,
An' legs tied down before they're cold –
   These are the things which make you know.

Also Time runnin' into years –
   A thousand Places left be'ind –
An' Men from both two 'emispheres
   Discussin' things of every kind;
So much more near than I 'ad known,
   So much more great than I 'ad guessed –
An' me, like all the rest, alone –
   But reachin' out to all the rest!

So 'ath it come to me – not pride,
   Nor yet conceit, but on the 'ole
(If such a term may be applied),
   The makin's of a bloomin' soul.

But now, discharged, I fall away
  To do with little things again . . .
Gawd, 'oo knows all I cannot say,
  Look after me in Thamesfontein![1]

If England was what England seems,
  An' not the England of our dreams,
But only putty, brass, an' paint,
  'Ow quick we'd chuck 'er! But she ain't!

[1] London.

'CITIES AND THRONES AND POWERS'

('A Centurion of the Thirtieth' –
Puck of Pook's Hill)

Cities and Thrones and Powers
  Stand in Time's eye,
Almost as long as flowers,
  Which daily die:
But, as new buds put forth
  To glad new men,
Out of the spent and unconsidered Earth
  The Cities rise again.

This season's Daffodil,
    She never hears
What change, what chance, what chill,
  Cut down last year's;
But with bold countenance,
  And knowledge small,
Esteems her seven days' continuance
  To be perpetual.

So Time that is o'er-kind
  To all that be,
Ordains us e'en as blind,
  As bold as she:
That in our very death,
  And burial sure,
Shadow to shadow, well persuaded, saith,
  'See how our works endure!'

THE RECALL

('An Habitation Enforced' –
Actions and Reactions)

I am the land of their fathers,
In me the virtue stays.
I will bring back my children,
After certain days.

Under their feet in the grasses
My clinging magic runs.
They shall return as strangers.
They shall remain as sons.

Over their heads in the branches
Of their new-bought, ancient trees,
I weave an incantation
And draw them to my knees.

Scent of smoke in the evening,
Smell of rain in the night –
The hours, the days and the seasons,
Order their souls aright,

Till I make plain the meaning
Of all my thousand years –
Till I fill their hearts with knowledge,
While I fill their eyes with tears.

PUCK'S SONG

(Enlarged from *Puck of Pook's Hill*)

See you the ferny ride that steals
Into the oak-woods far?
O that was whence they hewed the keels
That rolled to Trafalgar.

And mark you where the ivy clings
To Bayham's mouldering walls?
O there we cast the stout railings
That stand around St Paul's.

See you the dimpled track that runs
All hollow through the wheat?
O that was where they hauled the guns
That smote King Philip's fleet.

(Out of the Weald, the secret Weald,
Men sent in ancient years
The horse-shoes red at Flodden Field,
The arrows at Poitiers!)

See you our little mill that clacks,
So busy by the brook?
She has ground her corn and paid her tax
Ever since Domesday Book.

See you our stilly woods of oak,
And the dread ditch beside?
O that was where the Saxons broke
On the day that Harold died.

See you the windy levels spread
About the gates of Rye?
O that was where the Northmen fled,
When Alfred's ships came by.

See you our pastures wide and lone,
Where the red oxen browse?
O there was a City thronged and known,
Ere London boasted a house.

And see you, after rain, the trace
Of mound and ditch and wall?
O that was a Legion's camping-place,
When Caesar sailed from Gaul.

And see you marks that show and fade,
Like shadows on the Downs?
O they are the lines the Flint Men made,
To guard their wondrous towns.

Trackway and Camp and City lost,
Salt Marsh where now is corn –
Old Wars, old Peace, old Arts that cease,
And so was England born!

She is not any common Earth,
Water or wood or air,
But Merlin's Isle of Gramarye,
Where you and I will fare!

THE WAY THROUGH THE WOODS

('Marklake Witches' – *Rewards and Fairies*)

They shut the road through the woods
Seventy years ago.
Weather and rain have undone it again,
And now you would never know
There was once a road through the woods
Before they planted the trees.
It is underneath the coppice and heath
And the thin anemones.
Only the keeper sees
That, where the ring-dove broods,
And the badgers roll at ease,
There was once a road through the woods.

Yet, if you enter the woods
Of a summer evening late,
When the night-air cools on the trout-ringed pools
Where the otter whistles his mate,
(They fear not men in the woods,
Because they see so few.)
You will hear the beat of a horse's feet,
And the swish of a skirt in the dew,
Steadily cantering through
The misty solitudes,
As though they perfectly knew
The old lost road through the woods . . .
But there is no road through the woods.

A CHARM
(Introduction to *Rewards and Fairies*)

Take of English earth as much
As either hand may rightly clutch.
In the taking of it breathe
Prayer for all who lie beneath.
Not the great nor well-bespoke,
But the mere uncounted folk
Of whose life and death is none
Report or lamentation.
  Lay that earth upon thy heart,
  And thy sickness shall depart!

It shall sweeten and make whole
Fevered breath and festered soul.
It shall mightily restrain
Over-busied hand and brain.
It shall ease thy mortal strife
'Gainst the immortal woe of life,
Till thyself, restored, shall prove
By what grace the Heavens do move.

Take of English flowers these –
Spring's full-facèd primroses,
Summer's wild wide-hearted rose,
Autumn's wall-flower of the close,
And, thy darkness to illume,
Winter's bee-thronged ivy-bloom.
Seek and serve them where they bide
From Candlemas to Christmas-tide,
  For these simples, used aright,
  Can restore a failing sight.

A CHARM

These shall cleanse and purify
Webbed and inward-turning eye;
These shall show thee treasure hid
Thy familiar fields amid;
And reveal (which is thy need)
Every man a King indeed!

JOBSON'S AMEN
('In the Presence' – *A Diversity of Creatures*)

'Blessèd be the English and all their ways and works.
Cursèd be the Infidels, Hereticks, and Turks!'
'Amen,' quo' Jobson, 'but where I used to lie
Was neither Candle, Bell nor Book to curse my brethren by,

'But a palm-tree in full bearing, bowing down, bowing down,
To a surf that drove unsparing at the brown, walled town –
Conches in a temple, oil-lamps in a dome –
And a low moon out of Africa said: "This way home!"'

'Blessèd be the English and all that they profess.
Cursèd be the Savages that prance in nakedness!'
'Amen,' quo' Jobson, 'but where I used to lie
Was neither shirt nor pantaloons to catch my brethren by:

'But a well-wheel slowly creaking, going round, going round,
By a water-channel leaking over drowned, warm ground –
Parrots very busy in the trellised pepper-vine –
And a high sun over Asia shouting: "Rise and shine!"'

'Blessèd be the English and everything they own.
Cursèd be the Infidels that bow to wood and stone!'
'Amen,' quo' Jobson, 'but where I used to lie
Was neither pew nor Gospelleer to save my brethren by:

'But a desert stretched and stricken, left and right, left and right,
Where the piled mirages thicken under white-hot light –
A skull beneath a sand-hill and a viper coiled inside –
And a red wind out of Libya roaring: "Run and hide!"'

'Blessèd be the English and all they make or do.
Cursèd be the Hereticks who doubt that this is true!'
'Amen,' quo' Jobson, 'but where I mean to die
Is neither rule nor calliper to judge the matter by:

'But Himalaya heavenward-heading, sheer and vast, sheer and vast,
In a million summits bedding on the last world's past –
A certain sacred mountain where the scented cedars climb,
And – the feet of my Belovèd hurrying back through Time!'

'MY NEW-CUT ASHLAR'

(*L'Envoi* to *Life's Handicap*)

My new-cut ashlar takes the light
Where crimson-blank the windows flare.
By my own work before the night,
Great Overseer, I make my prayer.

If there be good in that I wrought
Thy Hand compelled it, Master, Thine –
Where I have failed to meet Thy Thought
I know, through Thee, the blame was mine.

One instant's toil to Thee denied
Stands all Eternity's offence.
Of that I did with Thee to guide,
To Thee, through Thee, be excellence.

The depth and dream of my desire,
The bitter paths wherein I stray –
Thou knowest Who hast made the Fire,
Thou knowest Who hast made the Clay.

Who, lest all thought of Eden fade,
Bring'st Eden to the craftsman's brain –
Godlike to muse o'er his own Trade
And manlike stand with God again!

One stone the more swings into place
In that dread Temple of Thy worth.
It is enough that, through Thy Grace,
I saw nought common on Thy Earth.

Take not that vision from my ken –
Oh, whatsoe'er may spoil or speed.
Help me to need no aid from men
That I may help such men as need!

THE NEW KNIGHTHOOD
('A Deal in Cotton' – *Actions and Reactions*)

Who gives him the Bath?
'I,' said the wet,
Rank Jungle-sweat,
'I'll give him the Bath!'

Who'll sing the psalms?
'We,' said the Palms.
'As the hot wind becalms,
'We'll sing the psalms.'

Who lays on the sword?
'I,' said the Sun,
'Before he has done,
'I'll lay on the sword.'

Who fastens his belt?
'I,' said Short-Rations,
'I know all the fashions
'Of tightening a belt!'

Who gives him his spur?
'I,' said his Chief,
Exacting and brief,
'I'll give him the spur.'

Who'll shake his hand?
'I,' said the Fever,
'And I'm no deceiver,
'I'll shake his hand.'

Who brings him the wine?
'I,' said Quinine,
'It's a habit of mine.
'*I*'ll come with his wine.'

Who'll put him to proof?
'I,' said All Earth.
'Whatever he's worth,
'I'll put to the proof.'

Who'll choose him for Knight?
'I,' said his Mother,
'Before any other,
'My very own Knight.'

And after this fashion, adventure to seek,
Was Sir Galahad made – as it might be last week!

HARP SONG OF THE DANE WOMEN

('The Knights of the Joyous Venture' –
Puck of Pook's Hill)

What is a woman that you forsake her,
And the hearth-fire and the home-acre,
To go with the old grey Widow-maker?

She has no house to lay a guest in –
But one chill bed for all to rest in,
That the pale suns and the stray bergs nest in.

She has no strong white arms to fold you,
But the ten-times-fingering weed to hold you –
Out on the rocks where the tide has rolled you.

Yet, when the signs of summer thicken,
And the ice breaks, and the birch-buds quicken,
Yearly you turn from our side, and sicken –

Sicken again for the shouts and the slaughters.
You steal away to the lapping waters,
And look at your ship in her winter-quarters.

You forget our mirth, and talk at the tables,
The kine in the shed and the horse in the stables –
To pitch her sides and go over her cables.

Then you drive out where the storm-clouds swallow,
And the sound of your oar-blades, falling hollow,
Is all we have left through the months to follow.

HARP SONG OF THE DANE WOMEN

Ah, what is Woman that you forsake her,
And the hearth-fire and the home-acre,
To go with the old grey Widow-maker?

THE PUZZLER

('The Puzzler' – *Actions and Reactions*)

The Celt in all his variants from Builth to Ballyhoo,
His mental processes are plain – one knows what he will do,
And can logically predicate his finish by his start;
But the English – ah, the English! – they are quite a race apart.

Their psychology is bovine, their outlook crude and raw.
They abandon vital matters to be tickled with a straw;
But the straw that they were tickled with – the chaff that they were
fed with –
They convert into a weaver's beam to break their foeman's head
with.

For undemocratic reasons and for motives not of State,
They arrive at their conclusions – largely inarticulate.
Being void of self-expression they confide their views to none;
But sometimes in a smoking-room, one learns why things were done.

Yes, sometimes in a smoking-room, through clouds of 'Ers' and
'Ums',
Obliquely and by inference, illumination comes,
On some step that they have taken, or some action they approve –
Embellished with the *argot* of the Upper Fourth Remove.

In telegraphic sentences, half nodded to their friends,
They hint a matter's inwardness – and there the matter ends.
And while the Celt is talking from Valencia to Kirkwall,
The English – ah, the English! – don't say anything at all.

HADRAMAUTI

(Enlarged from *Plain Tales from the Hills*)

Who knows the heart of the Christian? How does he reason?
What are his measures and balances? Which is his season
For laughter, forbearance or bloodshed, and what devils move him
When he arises to smite us? *I* do not love him.

He invites the derision of strangers – he enters all places.
Booted, bareheaded he enters. With shouts and embraces
He asks of us news of the household whom *we* reckon nameless.
Certainly Allah created him forty-fold shameless!

So it is not in the Desert. One came to me weeping –
The Avenger of Blood on his track – I took him in keeping.
Demanding not whom he had slain, I refreshed him, I fed him
As he were even a brother. But Eblis had bred him.

He was the son of an ape, ill at ease in his clothing.
He talked with his head, hands and feet. I endured him with loathing.
Whatever his spirit conceived his countenance showed it
As a frog shows in a mud-puddle. Yet I abode it!

I fingered my beard and was dumb, in silence confronting him.
His soul was too shallow for silence, e'en with Death hunting him.
I said: "'Tis his weariness speaks,' but, when he had rested,
He chirped in my face like some sparrow, and, presently, jested!

Wherefore slew I that stranger? He brought me dishonour.
I saddled my mare, Bijli, I set him upon her.

I gave him rice and goat's flesh. He bared me to laughter.
When he was gone from my tent, swift I followed after,
Taking my sword in my hand. The hot wine had filled him.
Under the stars he mocked me – therefore I killed him!

ROAD-SONG OF THE *BANDAR-LOG*

('Kaa's Hunting' – *The Jungle Book*)

Here we go in a flung festoon,
Half-way up to the jealous moon!
Don't you envy our pranceful bands?
Don't you wish you had extra hands?
Wouldn't you like if your tails were – *so* –
Curved in the shape of a Cupid's bow?
  Now you're angry, but – never mind,
  Brother, thy tail hangs down behind!

Here we sit in a branchy row,
Thinking of beautiful things we know;
Dreaming of deeds that we mean to do,
All complete, in a minute or two –
Something noble and grand and good,
Won by merely wishing we could.
  Now we're going to – never mind,
  Brother, thy tail hangs down behind!

All the talk we ever have heard
Uttered by bat or beast or bird –
Hide or fin or scale or feather –
Jabber it quickly and all together!
Excellent! Wonderful! Once again!
Now we are talking just like men.
  Let's pretend we are . . . Never mind!
  Brother, thy tail hangs down behind!
  This is the way of the Monkey-kind!

Then join our leaping lines that scumfish through the pines,
That rocket by where, light and high, the wild-grape swings.
By the rubbish in our wake, and the noble noise we make,
Be sure – be sure, we're going to do some splendid things!

A PICT SONG
('The Winged Hats' – *Puck of Pook's Hill*)

Rome never looks where she treads.
  Always her heavy hooves fall
On our stomachs, our hearts or our heads;
  And Rome never heeds when we bawl.
Her sentries pass on – that is all,
  And we gather behind them in hordes,
And plot to reconquer the Wall,
  With only our tongues for our swords.

We are the Little Folk – we!
  Too little to love or to hate.
Leave us alone and you'll see
  How we can drag down the State!
We are the worm in the wood!
  We are the rot at the root!
We are the taint in the blood!
  We are the thorn in the foot!

Mistletoe killing an oak –
  Rats gnawing cables in two –
Moths making holes in a cloak –
  How they must love what they do!
Yes – and we Little Folk too,
  We are busy as they –
Working our works out of view –
  Watch, and you'll see it some day!

No indeed! We are not strong,
  But we know Peoples that are.

Yes, and we'll guide them along
  To smash and destroy you in War!
We shall be slaves just the same?
  Yes, we have always been slaves,
But you – you will die of the shame,
  And then we shall dance on your graves!

We are the Little Folk, we, etc.

THE VOORTREKKER

The gull shall whistle in his wake, the blind wave break in fire.
He shall fulfil God's utmost will, unknowing His desire.
And he shall see old planets change and alien stars arise,
And give the gale his seaworn sail in shadow of new skies.
Strong lust of gear shall drive him forth and hunger arm his hand,
To win his food from the desert rude, his pittance from the sand.
His neighbours' smoke shall vex his eyes, their voices break his rest.
He shall go forth till south is north, sullen and dispossessed.
He shall desire loneliness and his desire shall bring,
Hard on his heels, a thousand wheels, a People and a King.
He shall come back on his own track, and by his scarce-cooled camp
There shall he meet the roaring street, the derrick and the stamp:
There he shall blaze a nation's ways with hatchet and with brand,
Till on his last-won wilderness an Empire's outposts stand!

A SCHOOL SONG

(Prelude to *Stalky & Co.*)

'Let us now praise famous men' –
Men of little showing –
For their work continueth,
And their work continueth,
Broad and deep continueth,
Greater than their knowing!

Western wind and open surge
Took us from our mothers –
Flung us on a naked shore
(Twelve bleak houses by the shore!
Seven summers by the shore!)
'Mid two hundred brothers.

There we met with famous men
Set in office o'er us;
And they beat on us with rods –
Faithfully with many rods –
Daily beat us on with rods,
For the love they bore us!

Out of Egypt unto Troy –
Over Himalaya –
Far and sure our bands have gone –
Hy-Brazil or Babylon,
Islands of the Southern Run,
And Cities of Cathaia!

And we all praise famous men –
  Ancients of the College;
For they taught us common sense –
Tried to teach us common sense –
Truth and God's Own Common Sense,
  Which is more than knowledge!

Each degree of Latitude
  Strung about Creation
Seeth one or more of us
(Of one muster each of us),
Diligent in that he does,
  Keen in his vocation.

This we learned from famous men,
  Knowing not its uses,
When they showed, in daily work,
Man must finish off his work –
Right or wrong, his daily work –
  And without excuses.

Servants of the Staff and chain,
  Mine and fuse and grapnel –
Some, before the face of Kings,
Stand before the face of Kings;
Bearing gifts to divers Kings –
  Gifts of case and shrapnel.

This we learned from famous men
  Teaching in our borders,
Who declarèd it was best,
Safest, easiest, and best –
Expeditious, wise, and best –
  To obey your orders.

Some beneath the further stars
  Bear the greater burden:
Set to serve the lands they rule,
(Save he serve no man may rule),
Serve and love the lands they rule;
  Seeking praise nor guerdon.

This we learned from famous men,
  Knowing not we learned it.
Only, as the years went by –
Lonely, as the years went by –
Far from help as years went by,
  Plainer we discerned it.

Wherefore praise we famous men
  From whose bays we borrow –
They that put aside To-day –
All the joys of their To-day –
And with toil of their To-day
  Bought for us To-morrow!

Bless and praise we famous men –
  Men of little showing –
For their work continueth,
And their work continueth,
Broad and deep continueth,
  Great beyond their knowing!

THE LAW OF THE JUNGLE
('How Fear Came' – *The Second Jungle Book*)

Now this is the Law of the Jungle – as old and as true as the sky;
And the Wolf that shall keep it may prosper, but the Wolf that shall break it must die.

As the creeper that girdles the tree-trunk the Law runneth forward and back –
For the strength of the Pack is the Wolf, and the strength of the Wolf is the Pack.

Wash daily from nose-tip to tail-tip; drink deeply, but never too deep;
And remember the night is for hunting, and forget not the day is for sleep.

The Jackal may follow the Tiger, but, Cub, when thy whiskers are grown,
Remember the Wolf is a hunter – go forth and get food of thine own.

Keep peace with the Lords of the Jungle – the Tiger, the Panther, the Bear;
And trouble not Hathi the Silent, and mock not the Boar in his lair.

When Pack meets with Pack in the Jungle, and neither will go from the trail,
Lie down till the leaders have spoken – it may be fair words shall prevail.

When ye fight with a Wolf of the Pack, ye must fight him alone and
afar,
Lest others take part in the quarrel, and the Pack be diminished by
war.

The Lair of the Wolf is his refuge, and where he has made him his
home,
Not even the Head Wolf may enter, not even the Council may come.

The Lair of the Wolf is his refuge, but where he has digged it too
plain,
The Council shall send him a message, and so he shall change it
again.

If ye kill before midnight, be silent, and wake not the woods with
your bay,
Lest ye frighten the deer from the crops, and the brothers go empty
away.

Ye may kill for yourselves, and your mates, and your cubs as they
need, and ye can;
But kill not for pleasure of killing, and *seven times never kill Man!*

If ye plunder his Kill from a weaker, devour not all in thy pride;
Pack-Right is the right of the meanest; so leave him the head and the
hide.

The Kill of the Pack is the meat of the Pack. Ye must eat where it
lies;
And no one may carry away of that meat to his lair, or he dies.

The Kill of the Wolf is the meat of the Wolf. He may do what he
will,
But, till he has given permission, the Pack may not eat of that Kill.

Cub-Right is the right of the Yearling. From all of his Pack he may
claim
Full-gorge when the killer has eaten; and none may refuse him the
same.

Lair-Right is the right of the Mother. From all of her year she may
claim
One haunch of each kill for her litter; and none may deny her the
same.

Cave-Right is the right of the Father – to hunt by himself for his
own:
He is freed of all calls to the Pack; he is judged by the Council alone.

Because of his age and his cunning, because of his gripe and his paw,
In all that the Law leaveth open, the word of the Head Wolf is Law.

Now these are the Laws of the Jungle, and many and mighty are they;
But the head and the hoof of the Law and the haunch and the hump is –
Obey!

THE CHILDREN'S SONG

(Puck of Pook's Hill)

Land of our Birth, we pledge to thee
Our love and toil in the years to be;
When we are grown and take our place
As men and women with our race.

Father in Heaven who lovest all,
Oh, help Thy children when they call;
That they may build from age to age
An undefilèd heritage.

Teach us to bear the yoke in youth,
With steadfastness and careful truth;
That, in our time, Thy Grace may give
The Truth whereby the Nations live.

Teach us to rule ourselves alway,
Controlled and cleanly night and day;
That we may bring, if need arise,
No maimed or worthless sacrifice.

Teach us to look in all our ends
On Thee for judge, and not our friends;
That we, with Thee, may walk uncowed
By fear or favour of the crowd.

Teach us the Strength that cannot seek,
By deed or thought, to hurt the weak;
That, under Thee, we may possess
Man's strength to comfort man's distress.

Teach us Delight in simple things,
And Mirth that has no bitter springs;
Forgiveness free of evil done,
And Love to all men 'neath the sun!

Land of our Birth, our faith, our pride,
For whose dear sake our fathers died;
Oh, Motherland, we pledge to thee
Head, heart, and hand through the years to be!

IF –

('Brother Square-Toes' – *Rewards and Fairies*)

If you can keep your head when all about you
Are losing theirs and blaming it on you,
If you can trust yourself when all men doubt you,
But make allowance for their doubting too;
If you can wait and not be tired by waiting,
Or being lied about, don't deal in lies,
Or being hated, don't give way to hating,
And yet don't look too good, nor talk too wise:

If you can dream – and not make dreams your master;
If you can think – and not make thoughts your aim;
If you can meet with Triumph and Disaster
And treat those two impostors just the same;
If you can bear to hear the truth you've spoken
Twisted by knaves to make a trap for fools,
Or watch the things you gave your life to, broken,
And stoop and build 'em up with worn-out tools:

If you can make one heap of all your winnings
And risk it on one turn of pitch-and-toss,
And lose, and start again at your beginnings
And never breathe a word about your loss;
If you can force your heart and nerve and sinew
To serve your turn long after they are gone,
And so hold on when there is nothing in you
Except the Will which says to them: 'Hold on!'

If you can talk with crowds and keep your virtue,
Or walk with Kings – nor lose the common touch,

If neither foes nor loving friends can hurt you,
  If all men count with you, but none too much;
If you can fill the unforgiving minute
  With sixty seconds' worth of distance run,
Yours is the Earth and everything that's in it,
  And – which is more – you'll be a Man, my son!

THE PRODIGAL SON

WESTERN VERSION

(Enlarged from *Kim*)

Here come I to my own again,
Fed, forgiven and known again,
Claimed by bone of my bone again
And cheered by flesh of my flesh.
The fatted calf is dressed for me,
But the husks have greater zest for me.
I think my pigs will be best for me,
So I'm off to the Yards afresh.

I never was very refined, you see,
(And it weighs on my brother's mind, you see)
But there's no reproach among swine, d'you see,
For being a bit of a swine.
So I'm off with wallet and staff to eat
The bread that is three parts chaff to wheat,
But glory be! – there's a laugh to it,
Which isn't the case when we dine.

My father glooms and advises me,
My brother sulks and despises me,
And Mother catechises me
Till I want to go out and swear.
And, in spite of the butler's gravity,
I know that the servants have it I
Am a monster of moral depravity,
And I'm damned if I think it's fair!

I wasted my substance, I know I did,
On riotous living, so I did,
But there's nothing on record to show I did
More than my betters have done.
They talk of the money I spent out there –
They hint at the pace that I went out there –
But they all forget I was sent out there
Alone as a rich man's son.

So I was a mark for plunder at once,
And lost my cash (can you wonder?) at once,
But I didn't give up and knock under at once.
I worked in the Yards, for a spell,
Where I spent my nights and my days with hogs,
And shared their milk and maize with hogs,
Till, I guess, I have learned what pays with hogs
And – I have that knowledge to sell!

So back I go to my job again,
Not so easy to rob again,
Or quite so ready to sob again
On any neck that's around.
I'm leaving, Pater. Good-bye to you!
God bless you, Mater! I'll write to you . . .
I wouldn't be impolite to you,
But, Brother, you *are* a Hound!

A TRANSLATION

HORACE, BK. V. ODE 3[1]

('Regulus' – *A Diversity of Creatures*)

There are whose study is of smells,
  And to attentive schools rehearse
How something mixed with something else
  Makes something worse.

Some cultivate in broths impure
  The clients of our body – these,
Increasing without Venus, cure,
  Or cause, disease.

Others the heated wheel extol,
  And all its offspring, whose concern
Is how to make it farthest roll
  And fastest turn.

Me, much incurious if the hour
  Present, or to be paid for, brings
Me to Brundusium by the power
  Of wheels or wings;

Me, in whose breast no flame hath burned
  Life-long, save that by Pindar lit,
Such lore leaves cold. I am not turned
  Aside to it

More than when, sunk in thought profound
  Of what the unaltering Gods require,
My steward (friend but slave) brings round
  Logs for my fire.

[1] A book of Horace entirely invented by Kipling. (Ed.)

OLD MOTHER LAIDINWOOL
(Enlarged from Old Song)

Old Mother Laidinwool had nigh twelve months been dead.
She heard the hops was doing well, an' so popped up her head,
For said she: 'The lads I've picked with when I was young and fair,
They're bound to be at hopping and I'm bound to meet 'em there!'

Let me up and go
Back to the work I know, Lord!
Back to the work I know, Lord!
For it's dark where I lie down, My Lord!
An' it's dark where I lie down!

Old Mother Laidinwool, she give her bones a shake,
An' trotted down the churchyard-path as fast as she could make.
She met the Parson walking, but she says to him, says she: –
'Oh, don't let no one trouble for a poor old ghost like me!'

'Twas all a warm September an' the hops had flourished grand.
She saw the folks get into 'em with stockin's on their hands;
An' none of 'em was foreigners but all which she had known,
And old Mother Laidinwool she blessed 'em every one.

She saw her daughters picking an' their children them-beside,
An' she moved among the babies an' she stilled 'em when they cried.
She saw their clothes was bought, not begged, an' they was clean an' fat,
An' Old Mother Laidinwool she thanked the Lord for that.

Old Mother Laidinwool she waited on all day
Until it come too dark to see an' people went away –
Until it come too dark to see an' lights began to show,
An' old Mother Laidinwool she hadn't where to go.

Old Mother Laidinwool she give her bones a shake,
An' trotted back to churchyard-mould as fast as she could make.
She went where she was bidden to an' there laid down her ghost . . .
An' the Lord have mercy on you in the Day you need it most!

Let me in again,
Out of the wet an' rain, Lord!
Out of the wet an' rain, Lord!
For it's best as You shall say, My Lord!
An' it's best as You shall say!

THE LAND

('Friendly Brook' – *A Diversity of Creatures*)

When Julius Fabricius, Sub-Prefect of the Weald,
In the days of Diocletian owned our Lower River-field,
He called to him Hobdenius – a Briton of the Clay,
Saying: 'What about that River-piece for layin' in to hay?'

And the aged Hobden answered: 'I remember as a lad
My father told your father that she wanted dreenin' bad.
An' the more that you neeglect her the less you'll get her clean.
Have it jest *as* you've a mind to, but, if I was you, I'd dreen.'

So they drained it long and crossways in the lavish Roman style –
Still we find among the river-drift their flakes of ancient tile,
And in drouthy middle August, when the bones of meadows show,
We can trace the lines they followed sixteen hundred years ago.

Then Julius Fabricius died as even Prefects do,
And after certain centuries, Imperial Rome died too.
Then did robbers enter Britain from across the Northern main
And our Lower River-field was won by Ogier the Dane.

Well could Ogier work his war-boat – well could Ogier wield his
brand –
Much he knew of foaming waters – not so much of farming land.
So he called to him a Hobden of the old unaltered blood,
Saying: 'What about that River-piece; she doesn't look no good?'

And that aged Hobden answered: ''Tain't for *me* to interfere,
But I've known that bit o' meadow now for five and fifty year.
Have it *jest* as you've a mind to, but I've proved it time on time,
If you want to change her nature you have *got* to give her lime!'

Ogier sent his wains to Lewes, twenty hours' solemn walk,
And drew back great abundance of the cool, grey, healing chalk.
And old Hobden spread it broadcast, never heeding what was in 't –
Which is why in cleaning ditches, now and then we find a flint.

Ogier died. His sons grew English – Anglo-Saxon was their name –
Till out of blossomed Normandy another pirate came;
For Duke William conquered England and divided with his men,
And our Lower River-field he gave to William of Warenne.

But the Brook (you know her habit) rose one rainy autumn night
And tore down sodden flitches of the bank to left and right.
So, said William to his Bailiff as they rode their dripping rounds:
'Hob, what about that River-bit – the Brook's got up no bounds?'

And that aged Hobden answered: "Tain't my business to advise,
But ye might ha' known 'twould happen from the way the valley lies.
Where ye can't hold back the water you must try and save the sile.
Hev it jest as you've a *mind* to, but, if I was you, I'd spile!'

They spiled along the water-course with trunks of willow-trees,
And planks of elms behind 'em and immortal oaken knees.
And when the spates of Autumn whirl the gravel-beds away
You can see their faithful fragments, iron-hard in iron clay.

. . . .

Georgii Quinti Anno Sexto, I, who own the River-field,
Am fortified with title-deeds, attested, signed and sealed,
Guaranteeing me, my assigns, my executors and heirs
All sorts of powers and profits which – are neither mine nor theirs.

I have rights of chase and warren, as my dignity requires.
I can fish – but Hobden tickles. I can shoot – but Hobden wires.
I repair, but he reopens, certain gaps which, men allege,
Have been used by every Hobden since a Hobden swapped a hedge.

Shall I dog his morning progress o'er the track-betraying dew?
Demand his dinner-basket into which my pheasant flew?
Confiscate his evening faggot under which my conies ran,
And summons him to judgment? I would sooner summons Pan.

His dead are in the churchyard – thirty generations laid.
Their names were old in history when Domesday Book was made;
And the passion and the piety and prowess of his line
Have seeded, rooted, fruited in some land the Law calls mine.

Not for any beast that burrows, not for any bird that flies,
Would I lose his large sound counsel, miss his keen amending eyes.
He is bailiff, woodman, wheelwright, field-surveyor, engineer,
And if flagrantly a poacher – 'tain't for me to interfere.

'Hob, what about that River-bit?' I turn to him again,
With Fabricius and Ogier and William of Warenne.
'Hev it jest as you've a mind to, *but*' – and here he takes command.
For whoever pays the taxes old Mus' Hobden owns the land.

JUST SO VERSES

When the cabin port-holes are dark and green
  Because of the seas outside;
When the ship goes *wop* (with a wiggle between)
And the steward falls into the soup-tureen,
  And the trunks begin to slide;
When Nursey lies on the floor in a heap,
And Mummy tells you to let her sleep,
And you aren't waked or washed or dressed,
Why, then you will know (if you haven't guessed)
You're 'Fifty North and Forty West'!

How the Whale Got his Throat.

. .

The Camel's hump is an ugly lump
  Which well you may see at the Zoo;
But uglier yet is the hump we get
  From having too little to do.

Kiddies and grown-ups too-oo-oo,
If we haven't enough to do-oo-oo,
    We get the hump –
    Cameelious hump –
The hump that is black and blue!

We climb out of bed with a frouzly head,
  And a snarly-yarly voice.
We shiver and scowl and we grunt and we growl
  At our bath and our boots and our toys;

And there ought to be a corner for me
(And I know there is one for you)
When we get the hump –
Cameelious hump –
The hump that is black and blue!

The cure for this ill is not to sit still,
Or frowst with a book by the fire;
But to take a large hoe and a shovel also,
And dig till you gently perspire;

And then you will find that the sun and the wind,
And the Djinn of the Garden too,
Have lifted the hump –
The horrible hump –
The hump that is black and blue!

I get it as well as you-oo-oo
If I haven't enough to do-oo-oo!
We all get hump –
Cameelious hump –
Kiddies and grown-ups too!

How the Camel Got his Hump.

. . .

I am the Most Wise Baviaan, saying in most wise tones,
'Let us melt into the landscape – just us two by our lones.'
People have come – in a carriage – calling. But Mummy is there . . .
Yes, I can go if you take me – Nurse says *she* don't care.
Let's go up to the pig-styes and sit on the farmyard rails!
Let's say things to the bunnies, and watch 'em skitter their tails!
Let's – oh, *anything*, daddy, so long as it's you and me,
And going truly exploring, and not being in till tea!

Here's your boots (I've brought 'em), and here's your cap and stick,
And here's your pipe and tobacco. Oh, come along out of it – quick!

How the Leopard Got his Spots.

. . .

I keep six honest serving-men
(They taught me all I knew);
Their names are What and Why and When
And How and Where and Who.
I send them over land and sea,
I send them east and west;
But after they have worked for me,
I give them all a rest.

I let them rest from nine till five,
For I am busy then,
As well as breakfast, lunch, and tea,
For they are hungry men.
But different folk have different views.
I know a person small –
She keeps ten million serving-men,
Who get no rest at all!

She sends 'em abroad on her own affairs,
From the second she opens her eyes –
One million Hows, two million Wheres,
And seven million Whys!

The Elephant's Child.

. . .

This is the mouth-filling song of the race that was run by a Boomer.
Run in a single burst – only event of its kind –
Started by Big God Nqong from Warrigaborrigarooma,
Old Man Kangaroo first, Yellow-Dog Dingo behind.

Kangaroo bounded away, his back-legs working like pistons –
Bounded from morning till dark, twenty-five feet at a bound.
Yellow-Dog Dingo lay like a yellow cloud in the distance –
Much too busy to bark. My! but they covered the ground!

Nobody knows where they went, or followed the track that they flew
in,
For that Continent hadn't been given a name.
They ran thirty degrees, from Torres Straits to the Leeuwin
(Look at the Atlas, please), then they ran back as they came.

S'posing you could trot from Adelaide to the Pacific,
For an afternoon's run – half what these gentlemen did –
You would feel rather hot, but your legs would develop terrific –
Yes, my importunate son, you'd be a Marvellous Kid!

The Sing-Song of Old Man Kangaroo.

. . .

I've never sailed the Amazon,
I've never reached Brazil;
But the *Don* and *Magdalena*,
They can go there when they will!

Yes, weekly from Southampton,
Great steamers, white and gold,
Go rolling down to Rio
(Roll down – roll down to Rio!).
And I'd like to roll to Rio
Some day before I'm old!

I've never seen a Jaguar,
Nor yet an Armadill-
o dilloing in his armour,
And I s'pose I never will,

Unless I go to Rio
These wonders to behold –
Roll down – roll down to Rio –
Roll really down to Rio!
Oh, I'd love to roll to Rio
Some day before I'm old!

The Beginning of the Armadilloes.

• •

China-going P. & O.'s
Pass Pau Amma's playground close,
And his Pusat Tasek lies
Near the track of most B.I.'s.
N.Y.K. and N.D.L.
Know Pau Amma's home as well
As the Fisher of the Sea knows
'Bens,' M.M.'s and Rubattinos.
But (and this is rather queer)
A.T.L.'s can *not* come here;
O. and O. and D.O.A.
Must go round another way.
Orient, Anchor, Bibby, Hall,
Never go that way at all.
U.C.S. would have a fit
If it found itself on it.
And if 'Beavers' took their cargoes
To Penang instead of Lagos,
Or a fat Shaw-Savill bore
Passengers to Singapore,
Or a White Star were to try a
Little trip to Sourabaya,
Or a B.S.A. went on
Past Natal to Cheribon,

Then great Mr Lloyds would come
With a wire and drag them home!

. . . . .

You'll know what my riddle means
When you've eaten mangosteens.

The Crab that Played with the Sea.

. . .

Pussy can sit by the fire and sing,
Pussy can climb a tree,
Or play with a silly old cork and string
To 'muse herself, not me.
But *I* like *Binkie* my dog, because
He knows how to behave;
So, *Binkie's* the same as the First Friend was,
And I am the Man in the Cave!

Pussy will play Man-Friday till
It's time to wet her paw
And make her walk on the window-sill
(For the footprint Crusoe saw);
Then she fluffles her tail and mews,
And scratches and won't attend.
But *Binkie* will play whatever I choose,
And he is my true First Friend!

Pussy will rub my knees with her head
Pretending she loves me hard;
But the very minute I go to my bed
Pussy runs out in the yard,
And there she stays till the morning-light;
So I know it is only pretend;

But *Binkie*, he snores at my feet all night,
And he is my Firstest Friend!
The Cat that Walked by Himself.

. . .

This Uninhabited Island
Is near Cape Gardafui;
But it's hot – too hot – off Suez
For the likes of you and me
Ever to go in a P. & O.
To call on the Cake Parsee.
How the Rhinoceros got his Skin.

. . .

There was never a Queen like Balkis,
From here to the wide world's end;
But Balkis talked to a butterfly
As you would talk to a friend.

There was never a King like Solomon,
Not since the world began;
But Solomon talked to a butterfly
As a man would talk to a man.

She was Queen of Sabaea –
And *he* was Asia's Lord –
But they both of 'em talked to butterflies
When they took their walks abroad!
The Butterfly that Stamped.

THE LOOKING-GLASS

A Country Dance

(Enlarged from *Rewards and Fairies*)

Queen Bess was Harry's daughter. Stand forward partners all!
In ruff and stomacher and gown
She danced King Philip down-a-down,
And left her shoe to show 'twas true –
(The very tune I'm playing you)
In Norgem at Brickwall![1]
The Queen was in her chamber, and she was middling old.
Her petticoat was satin, and her stomacher was gold.
Backwards and forwards and sideways did she pass,
Making up her mind to face the cruel looking-glass.
The cruel looking-glass that will never show a lass
As comely or as kindly or as young as what she was!

Queen Bess was Harry's daughter. Now hand your partners all!

The Queen was in her chamber, a-combing of her hair.
There came Queen Mary's spirit and It stood behind her chair,
Singing 'Backwards and forwards and sideways may you pass,
But I will stand behind you till you face the looking-glass.
The cruel looking-glass that will never show a lass
As lovely or unlucky or as lonely as I was!'

Queen Bess was Harry's daughter. Now turn your partners all!

The Queen was in her chamber, a-weeping very sore,
There came Lord Leicester's spirit and It scratched upon the door,

[1] A pair of Queen Elizabeth's shoes are still at Brickwall House, Northiam, Sussex.

Singing 'Backwards and forwards and sideways may you pass,
But I will walk beside you till you face the looking-glass.
The cruel looking-glass that will never show a lass,
As hard and unforgiving or as wicked as you was!'

Queen Bess was Harry's daughter. Now kiss your partners all!

The Queen was in her chamber, her sins were on her head.
She looked the spirits up and down and statelily she said:–
'Backwards and forwards and sideways though I've been,
Yet I am Harry's daughter and I am England's Queen!'
And she faced the looking-glass (and whatever else there was)
And she saw her day was over and she saw her beauty pass
In the cruel looking-glass, that can always hurt a lass
More hard than any ghost there is or any man there was!

A SMUGGLER'S SONG
('Hal o' the Draft' – *Puck of Pook's Hill*)

If you wake at midnight, and hear a horse's feet,
Don't go drawing back the blind, or looking in the street,
Them that asks no questions isn't told a lie.
Watch the wall, my darling, while the Gentlemen go by!
Five and twenty ponies
Trotting through the dark –
Brandy for the Parson,
'Baccy for the Clerk;
Laces for a lady, letters for a spy,
And watch the wall, my darling, while the Gentlemen go by!

Running round the woodlump if you chance to find
Little barrels, roped and tarred, all full of brandy-wine,
Don't you shout to come and look, nor use 'em for your play.
Put the brishwood back again – and they'll be gone next day!

If you see the stable-door setting open wide;
If you see a tired horse lying down inside;
If your mother mends a coat cut about and tore;
If the lining's wet and warm – don't you ask no more!

If you meet King George's men, dressed in blue and red,
You be careful what you say, and mindful what is said.
If they call you 'pretty maid', and chuck you 'neath the chin,
Don't you tell where no one is, nor yet where no one's been!

Knocks and footsteps round the house – whistles after dark –
You've no call for running out till the house-dogs bark.
Trusty's here, and *Pincher*'s here, and see how dumb they lie –
They don't fret to follow when the Gentlemen go by!

If you do as you've been told, 'likely there's a chance,
You'll be give a dainty doll, all the way from France,
With a cap of Valenciennes, and a velvet hood –
A present from the Gentlemen, along o' being good!

Five and twenty ponies
Trotting through the dark –
Brandy for the Parson,
'Baccy for the Clerk.

Them that asks no questions isn't told a lie –
Watch the wall, my darling, while the Gentlemen go by!

HERIOT'S FORD
(Enlarged from *The Light that Failed*)

'What's that that hirples at my side?'
The foe that you must fight, my lord.
'That rides as fast as I can ride?'
The shadow of your might, my lord.

'Then wheel my horse against the foe!'
He's down and overpast, my lord.
You war against the sunset-glow,
The judgment follows fast, my lord!

'Oh, who will stay the sun's descent?'
King Joshua he is dead, my lord.
'I need an hour to repent!'
'Tis what our sister said, my lord.

'Oh, do not slay me in my sins!'
You're safe awhile with us, my lord.
'Nay, kill me ere my fear begins!'
We would not serve you thus, my lord.

'Where is the doom that I must face?'
Three little leagues away, my lord.
'Then mend the horses' laggard pace!'
We need them for next day, my lord.

'Next day – next day! Unloose my cords!'
Our sister needed none, my lord.
You had no mind to face our swords,
And – where can cowards run, my lord?

'You would not kill the soul alive?'
'Twas thus our sister cried, my lord.
'I dare not die with none to shrive.'
But so our sister died, my lord.

'Then wipe the sweat from brow and cheek.'
It runnels forth afresh, my lord.
'Uphold me – for the flesh is weak.'
You've finished with the Flesh, my lord!

SONG OF THE GALLEY-SLAVES

('"The Finest Story in the World"' – *Many Inventions*)

We pulled for you when the wind was against us and the sails were low.

Will you never let us go?

We ate bread and onions when you took towns, or ran aboard quickly when you were beaten back by the foe.

The Captains walked up and down the deck in fair weather singing songs, but we were below.

We fainted with our chins on the oars and you did not see that we were idle, for we still swung to and fro.

Will you never let us go?

The salt made the oar-handles like shark-skin; our knees were cut to the bone with salt-cracks; our hair was stuck to our foreheads; and our lips were cut to the gums, and you whipped us because we could not row.

Will you never let us go?

But, in a little time, we shall run out of the port-holes as the water runs along the oar-blade, and though you tell the others to row after us you will never catch us till you catch the oar-thresh and tie up the winds in the belly of the sail. Aho!

Will you never let us go?

THE BEGINNINGS
1914–18
('Mary Postgate' – *A Diversity of Creatures*)

It was not part of their blood,
  It came to them very late
With long arrears to make good,
  When the English began to hate.

They were not easily moved,
  They were icy-willing to wait
Till every count should be proved,
  Ere the English began to hate.

Their voices were even and low,
  Their eyes were level and straight.
There was neither sign nor show,
  When the English began to hate.

It was not preached to the crowd,
  It was not taught by the State.
No man spoke it aloud,
  When the English began to hate.

It was not suddenly bred,
  It will not swiftly abate,
Through the chill years ahead,
  When Time shall count from the date
  That the English began to hate.

THE IDIOT BOY
(WORDSWORTH)

He wandered down the mountain grade
  Beyond the speed assigned –
A youth whom Justice often stayed
  And generally fined.

He went alone, that none might know
  If he could drive or steer.
Now he is in the ditch, and Oh!
  The differential gear!

(From *The Muse among the Motors*.)

NORMAN AND SAXON
(A.D. 1100)

'My son,' said the Norman Baron, 'I am dying, and you will be heir
To all the broad acres in England that William gave me for my share
When we conquered the Saxon at Hastings, and a nice little handful it is.
But before you go over to rule it I want you to understand this:–

'The Saxon is not like us Normans. His manners are not so polite.
But he never means anything serious till he talks about justice and right.
When he stands like an ox in the furrow with his sullen set eyes on your own,
And grumbles, "This isn't fair dealing," my son, leave the Saxon alone.

'You can horsewhip your Gascony archers, or torture your Picardy spears;
But don't try that game on the Saxon; you'll have the whole brood round your ears.
From the richest old Thane in the county to the poorest chained serf in the field,
They'll be at you and on you like hornets, and, if you are wise, you will yield.

'But first you must master their language, their dialect, proverbs and songs.
Don't trust any clerk to interpret when they come with the tale of their wrongs.

Let them know that you know what they're saying; let them feel
that you know what to say.
Yes, even when you want to go hunting, hear 'em out if it takes you
all day.

'They'll drink every hour of the daylight and poach every hour of
the dark.
It's the sport not the rabbits they're after (we've plenty of game in
the park).
Don't hang them or cut off their fingers. That's wasteful as well as
unkind,
For a hard-bitten, South-country poacher makes the best man-at-
arms you can find.

'Appear with your wife and the children at their weddings and
funerals and feasts.
Be polite but not friendly to Bishops; be good to all poor parish
priests.
Say "we", "us" and "ours" when you're talking, instead of "you
fellows" and "I".
Don't ride over seeds; keep your temper; and *never you tell 'em a lie!*'

THE SECRET OF THE MACHINES
(Modern Machinery)

We were taken from the ore-bed and the mine,
  We were melted in the furnace and the pit –
We were cast and wrought and hammered to design,
  We were cut and filed and tooled and gauged to fit.
Some water, coal, and oil is all we ask,
  And a thousandth of an inch to give us play:
And now, if you will set us to our task,
  We will serve you four and twenty hours a day!

    We can pull and haul and push and lift and drive,
    We can print and plough and weave and heat and light,
    We can run and race and swim and fly and dive,
    We can see and hear and count and read and write!

Would you call a friend from half across the world?
  If you'll let us have his name and town and state,
You shall see and hear your crackling question hurled
  Across the arch of heaven while you wait.
Has he answered? Does he need you at his side?
  You can start this very evening if you choose,
And take the Western Ocean in the stride
  Of seventy thousand horses and some screws!

    The boat-express is waiting your command!
    You will find the *Mauretania* at the quay,
    Till her captain turns the lever 'neath his hand,
    And the monstrous nine-decked city goes to sea.

Do you wish to make the mountains bare their head
  And lay their new-cut forests at your feet?
Do you want to turn a river in its bed,
  Or plant a barren wilderness with wheat?
Shall we pipe aloft and bring you water down
  From the never-failing cisterns of the snows,
To work the mills and tramways in your town,
  And irrigate your orchards as it flows?

It is easy! Give us dynamite and drills!
Watch the iron-shouldered rocks lie down and quake,
As the thirsty desert-level floods and fills,
And the valley we have dammed becomes a lake.

But remember, please, the Law by which we live,
  We are not built to comprehend a lie,
We can neither love nor pity nor forgive.
  If you make a slip in handling us you die!
We are greater than the Peoples or the Kings –
  Be humble, as you crawl beneath our rods! –
Our touch can alter all created things,
  We are everything on earth – except The Gods!

Though our smoke may hide the Heavens from your eyes,
It will vanish and the stars will shine again,
Because, for all our power and weight and size,
We are nothing more than children of your brain!

THE MASTER-COOK
('His Gift')

With us there rade a Maister-Cook that came
From the Rochelle whish is neere Angoulême.
Littel hee was, but rounder than a topp,
And his small berd hadde dipped in manie a soppe.
His honde was smoother than beseemeth mann's,
And his discoorse was all of marzipans,[1]
Of tripes of Caen, or Burdeux snailés swote,[2]
And Seinte Menhoulde wher cooken piggés-foote.[3]
To Thoulouse and to Bress and Carcasson
For pyes and fowles and chesnottes hadde hee wonne;[4]
Of hammés of Thuringie[5] colde hee prate,
And well hee knew what Princes hadde on plate
At Christmas-tide, from Artois to Gascogne.

Lordinges, quod hee, manne liveth nat alone
By bred, but meatés rost and seethed, and broth,
And purchasable[6] deinties, on mine othe.
Honey and hote gingere well liketh hee,
And whalés-flesch mortred[7] with spicerie.
For, lat be all how man denie or carpe,[8]

[1] A kind of sticky sweetmeat.

[2] Bordeaux snails are specially large and sweet.

[3] They grill pigs' feet still at St Menehoulde, not far from Verdun, better than anywhere else in all the world.

[4] Gone – to get pâtés of ducks' liver at Toulouse; fatted poultry at Bourg in Bresse, on the road to Geneva; and very large chestnuts in sugar at Carcassonne, about forty miles from Toulouse.

[5] This would probably be some sort of wild-boar ham from Germany.

[6] Expensive. [7] Beaten up. [8] Sneer or despise.

Him thries a daie his honger maketh sharpe,
And setteth him at boorde[1] with hawkés eyne,
Snuffing what dish is set beforne to deyne,
Nor, till with meate he all-to fill to brim,
None other matter nowher mooveth him.
Lat holie Seintés sterve[2] as bookés boast,
Most mannés soule is in his bellie most.
For, as man thinketh in his hearte is hee,
But, as hee eateth so his thought shall bee.
And Holie Fader's self[3] (with reveraunce)
Oweth to Cooke his port and his presaunce.
Wherbye it cometh past disputison[4]
Cookes over alle men have dominion,
Which follow them as schippe her gouvernail.[5]
Enoff of wordes – beginneth heere my tale:–

[1] Brings him to table. [2] Starve.

[3] The Pope himself, who depends on his cook for being healthy and well-fed.

[4] Dispute or argument.

[5] Men are influenced by their cooks as ships are steered by their rudders.

WE AND THEY
('A Friend of the Family')

Father, Mother, and Me,
  Sister and Auntie say
All the people like us are We,
  And every one else is They.
And They live over the sea,
  While We live over the way,
But – would you believe it? – They look upon We
  As only a sort of They!

We eat pork and beef
  With cow-horn-handled knives.
They who gobble Their rice off a leaf,
  Are horrified out of Their lives;
While They who live up a tree,
  And feast on grubs and clay,
(Isn't it scandalous?) look upon We
  As a simply disgusting They!

We shoot birds with a gun.
  They stick lions with spears.
Their full-dress is un-.
  We dress up to Our ears.
They like Their friends for tea,
  We like Our friends to stay;
And, after all that, They look upon We
  As an utterly ignorant They!

We eat kitcheny food.
  We have doors that latch.

They drink milk or blood,
  Under an open thatch.
We have Doctors to fee.
  They have Wizards to pay.
And (impudent heathen!) They look upon We
  As a quite impossible They!

All good people agree,
  And all good people say,
All nice people, like Us, are We
  And every one else is They:
But if you cross over the sea,
  Instead of over the way,
You may end by (think of it!) looking on We
  As only a sort of They!

THE LAST ODE

NOV. 27, 8 B.C.

HORACE, BK. V. ODE 31

('The Eye of Allah')

As watchers couched beneath a Bantine oak,
  Hearing the dawn-wind stir,
Know that the present strength of night is broke
  Though no dawn threaten her
Till dawn's appointed hour – so Virgil died,
Aware of change at hand, and prophesied

Change upon all the Eternal Gods had made
  And on the Gods alike –
Fated as dawn but, as the dawn, delayed
  Till the just hour should strike –

A Star new-risen above the living and dead;
  And the lost shades that were our loves restored
As lovers, and for ever. So he said;
  Having received the word . . .

Maecenas waits me on the Esquiline:
  Thither to-night go I . . .
And shall this dawn restore us, Virgil mine,
  To dawn? Beneath what sky?

THE DISCIPLE
('The Church that was at Antioch')

He that hath a Gospel
  To loose upon Mankind,
Though he serve it utterly –
  Body, soul and mind –
Though he go to Calvary
  Daily for its gain –
It is His Disciple
  Shall make his labour vain.

He that hath a Gospel
  For all earth to own –
Though he etch it on the steel,
  Or carve it on the stone –
Not to be misdoubted
  Through the after-days –
It is His Disciple
  Shall read it many ways.

It is His Disciple
  (Ere Those Bones are dust)
Who shall change the Charter,
  Who shall split the Trust –
Amplify distinctions,
  Rationalise the Claim;
Preaching that the Master
  Would have done the same.

It is His Disciple
  Who shall tell us how

Much the Master would have scrapped
  Had he lived till now –
What he would have modified
  Of what he said before.
It is His Disciple
  Shall do this and more . . .

He that hath a Gospel
  Whereby Heaven is won
(Carpenter, or cameleer,
  Or Maya's dreaming son),
Many swords shall pierce Him,
  Mingling blood with gall;
But His Own Disciple
  Shall wound Him worst of all!

THE GODS OF THE COPYBOOK HEADINGS

1919

As I pass through my incarnations in every age and race,
I make my proper prostrations to the Gods of the Market-Place.
Peering through reverent fingers I watch them flourish and fall,
And the Gods of the Copybook Headings, I notice, outlast them all.

We were living in trees when they met us. They showed us each in turn
That Water would certainly wet us, as Fire would certainly burn:
But we found them lacking in Uplift, Vision and Breadth of Mind,
So we left them to teach the Gorillas while we followed the March of Mankind.

We moved as the Spirit listed. *They* never altered their pace,
Being neither cloud nor wind-borne like the Gods of the Market-Place;
But they always caught up with our progress, and presently word would come
That a tribe had been wiped off its icefield, or the lights had gone out in Rome.

With the Hopes that our World is built on they were utterly out of touch,
They denied that the Moon was Stilton; they denied she was even Dutch.
They denied that Wishes were Horses; they denied that a Pig had Wings.
So we worshipped the Gods of the Market Who promised these beautiful things.

When the Cambrian measures were forming, They promised perpetual peace.
They swore, if we gave them our weapons, that the wars of the tribes would cease.
But when we disarmed They sold us and delivered us bound to our foe,
And the Gods of the Copybook Headings said: '*Stick to the Devil you know.*'

On the first Feminian Sandstones we were promised the Fuller Life
(Which started by loving our neighbour and ended by loving his wife)
Till our women had no more children and the men lost reason and faith,
And the Gods of the Copybook Headings said: '*The Wages of Sin is Death.*'

In the Carboniferous Epoch we were promised abundance for all,
By robbing selected Peter to pay for collective Paul;
But, though we had plenty of money, there was nothing our money could buy,
And the Gods of the Copybook Headings said: '*If you don't work you die.*'

Then the Gods of the Market tumbled, and their smooth-tongued wizards withdrew,
And the hearts of the meanest were humbled and began to believe it was true
That All is not Gold that Glitters, and Two and Two make Four –
And the Gods of the Copybook Headings limped up to explain it once more.

. . . .

As it will be in the future, it was at the birth of Man –
There are only four things certain since Social Progress began:
That the Dog returns to his Vomit and the Sow returns to her Mire,
And the burnt Fool's bandaged finger goes wabbling back to the
  Fire;

And that after this is accomplished, and the brave new world begins
When all men are paid for existing and no man must pay for his sins,
As surely as Water will wet us, as surely as Fire will burn,
The Gods of the Copybook Headings with terror and slaughter
  return!

THE CLERKS AND THE BELLS

(Oxford in 1920)

The merry clerks of Oxenford they stretch themselves at ease
Unhelmeted on unbleached sward beneath unshrivelled trees.
For the leaves, the leaves, are on the bough, the bark is on the bole,
And East and West men's housen stand all even-roofed and whole . . .
(*Men's housen doored and glazed and floored and whole at every turn!*)
And so the Bells of Oxenford ring:– 'Time it is to learn!'

The merry clerks of Oxenford they read and they are told
Of famous men who drew the sword in furious fights of old.
They heark and mark it faithfully, but never clerk will write
What vision rides 'twixt book and eye from any nearer fight.
(*Whose supplication rends the soul? Whose night-long cries repeat?*)
And so the Bells of Oxenford ring:– 'Time it is to eat!'

The merry clerks of Oxenford they sit them down anon
At tables fair with silver-ware and naperies thereon,
Free to refuse or dainty choose what dish shall seem them good;
For they have done with single meats, and waters streaked with
blood . . .
(*That three days' fast is overpast when all those guns said 'Nay'!*)
And so the Bells of Oxenford ring:– 'Time it is to play!'

The merry clerks of Oxenford they hasten one by one
Or band in companies abroad to ride, or row, or run
By waters level with fair meads all goldenly bespread,
Where flash June's clashing dragon-flies – but no man bows his
head,
(*Though bullet-wise June's dragon-flies deride the fearless air!*)
And so the Bells of Oxenford ring:– 'Time it is for prayer!'

The pious clerks of Oxenford they kneel at twilight-tide
For to receive and well believe the Word of Him Who died.
And, though no present wings of Death hawk hungry round that
  place,
Their brows are bent upon their hands that none may see their
  face –
(*Who set aside the world and died? What life shall please Him best?*)
And so the Bells of Oxenford ring:– 'Time it is to rest!'

The merry clerks of Oxenford lie under bolt and bar
Lest they should rake the midnight clouds or chase a sliding star.
In fear of fine and dread rebuke, they round their full-night sleep,
And leave that world which once they took for older men to keep.
(*Who walks by dreams what ghostly wood in search of playmate slain?*)
Until the Bells of Oxenford ring in the light again.

Unburdened breeze, unstricken trees, and all God's works restored –
In this way live the merry clerks – the clerks of Oxenford!

'HIS APOLOGIES'
1932

Master, this is Thy Servant. He is rising eight weeks old.
He is mainly Head and Tummy. His legs are uncontrolled.
But Thou hast forgiven his ugliness, and settled him on Thy knee . . .
Art Thou content with Thy Servant? He is *very* comfy with Thee.

Master, behold a Sinner! He hath committed a wrong.
He hath defiled Thy Premises through being kept in too long.
Wherefore his nose has been rubbed in the dirt, and his self-respect
has been bruisèd.
Master, pardon Thy Sinner, and see he is properly loosèd.

Master – again Thy Sinner! This that was once Thy Shoe,
He has found and taken and carried aside, as fitting matter to chew.
Now there is neither blacking nor tongue, and the Housemaid has
us in tow.
Master, remember Thy Servant is young, and tell her to let him go!

Master, extol Thy Servant, he has met a most Worthy Foe!
There has been fighting all over the Shop – and into the Shop also!
Till cruel umbrellas parted the strife (or I might have been choking
him yet),
But Thy Servant has had the Time of his Life – and now shall we
call on the vet?

Master, behold Thy Servant! Strange children came to play,
And because they fought to caress him, Thy Servant wentedst away.
But now that the Little Beasts have gone, he has returned to see
(Brushed – with his Sunday collar on) what they left over from tea.

. . . .

Master, pity Thy Servant! He is deaf and three parts blind.
He cannot catch Thy Commandments. He cannot read Thy Mind.
Oh, leave him not to his loneliness; nor make him that kitten's scorn.
He hath had none other God than Thee since the year that he was born.

Lord, look down on Thy Servant! Bad things have come to pass.
There is no heat in the midday sun, nor health in the wayside grass.
His bones are full of an old disease – his torments run and increase.
Lord, make haste with Thy Lightnings and grant him a quick release!

THE STORM CONE
1932

This is the midnight – let no star
Delude us – dawn is very far.
This is the tempest long foretold –
Slow to make head but sure to hold.

Stand by! The lull 'twixt blast and blast
Signals the storm is near, not past;
And worse than present jeopardy
May our forlorn to-morrow be.

If we have cleared the expectant reef,
Let no man look for his relief.
Only the darkness hides the shape
Of further peril to escape.

It is decreed that we abide
The weight of gale against the tide
And those huge waves the outer main
Sends in to set us back again.

They fall and whelm. We strain to hear
The pulses of her labouring gear,
Till the deep throb beneath us proves,
After each shudder and check, she moves!

She moves, with all save purpose lost,
To make her offing from the coast;
But, till she fetches open sea,
Let no man deem that he is free!

THE APPEAL

If I have given you delight
  By aught that I have done,
Let me lie quiet in that night
  Which shall be yours anon:

And for the little, little, span
  The dead are borne in mind,
Seek not to question other than
  The books I leave behind.

INDEXES

INDEX OF TITLES

Absent-Minded Beggar, The, 210
Appeal, The, 302
Arithmetic on the Frontier, 13

'Back to the Army Again', 181
Ballad of Boh Da Thone, The, 104
Ballad of East and West, The, 99
Beginnings, The, 281
Belts, 171
Betrothed, The, 15
'Birds of Prey' March, 184
'Bobs', 155
Boots, 215
Broken Men, The, 40

Cells, 164
Chant-Pagan, 212
Charm, A, 231
Children's Song, The, 255
Cholera Camp, 191
'Cities and Thrones and Powers', 226
'City of Brass, The', 123
Clerks and the Bells, The, 297
Conundrum of the Workshops, The, 141

Danny Deever, 158
Dedication from *Barrack-Room Ballads*, 32
Disciple, The, 292
Dykes, The, 120

'Eathen, The, 203
English Flag, The, 95
Exiles' Line, The, 69
Explanation, The, 149

Female of the Species, The, 146
First Chantey, The, 67
'Follow me 'ome', 199
'For All We Have and Are', 132
'For to Admire', 208
Ford o' Kabul River, 177
'Fuzzy-Wuzzy', 162

Galley-Slave, The, 24
Gentlemen-Rankers, 179
Gethsemane, 43
Gods of the Copybook Headings, The, 294
Gunga Din, 166

Hadramauti, 242
Half-Ballade of Waterval, 221
Harp Song of the Dane Women, 239
Heriot's Ford, 278
'His Apologies', 299

Idiot Boy, The, 282
If –, 257
In the Neolithic Age, 143
Islanders, The, 116

Jobson's Amen, 233
Just So Verses, 267

King, The, 150

Ladies, The, 193
Land, The, 264

Last Ode, The, 291
Law of the Jungle, The, 252
L'Envoi, 31
Lesson, The, 114
Lichtenberg, 219
Long Trail, The, 72
Looking-Glass, The, 274

McAndrew's Hymn, 58
Mandalay, 173
Married Man, The, 217
'Mary, Pity Women!', 206
Master-Cook, The, 287
'Men that Fought at Minden, The', 189
Mother-Lodge, The, 196
'My New-Cut Ashlar', 235

New Knighthood, The, 237
Norman and Saxon, 283

Old Men, The, 126
Old Mother Laidinwool, 262
One Viceroy Resigns, 18
Our Lady of the Snows, 86
Overland Mail, The, 11

Pict Song, A, 246
Prodigal Son, The, 259
Puck's Song, 228
Puzzler, The, 241

Recall, The, 227
Recessional, 130
Return, The, 223
Rhodes Memorial, Table Mountain, 88
Rhyme of the Three Captains, The, 136

Rhyme of the Three Sealers, The, 50
Road-Song of the *Bandar-Log*, 244

School Song, A, 249
Sea and the Hills, The, 48
Sea-Wife, The, 38
Second Voyage, The, 65
Secret of the Machines, The, 285
Sergeant's Weddin', The, 201
Sestina of the Tramp-Royal, 34
Smuggler's Song, A, 276
'Soldier an' Sailor Too', 186
Song of the Banjo, The, 44
Song of the English, A, 76
Song of the Galley-Slaves, 280
Sons of Martha, The, 152
Storm Cone, The, 301
Sussex, 89

Tale of Two Cities, A, 26
Three-Decker, The, 134
Tommy, 160
Translation, A, 261
Troopin', 175
Two Months, 29

Vampire, The, 93
Voortrekker, The, 248

Way Through the Woods, The, 230
We and They, 289
When Earth's Last Picture is Painted, 98
'When 'Omer Smote 'is Bloomin' Lyre', 145
White Man's Burden, The, 128
Widow at Windsor, The, 169

Zion, 36

INDEX OF FIRST LINES

A fool there was and he made his prayer, 93
A great and glorious thing it is, 13
A Nation spoke to a Nation, 86
As I pass through my incarnations in every age and race, 294
As I was spittin' into the Ditch aboard o' the *Crocodile*, 186
As tho' again – yea, even once again, 88
As watchers couched beneath a Bantine oak, 291
. . . At the close of a winter day, 136
'Ave you 'eard o' the Widow at Windsor, 169
Away by the lands of the Japanee, 50

Beyond the path of the outmost sun through utter darkness hurled, 32
'Blessèd be the English and all their ways and works', 233
By the old Moulmein Pagoda, lookin' lazy at the sea, 173

Cities and Thrones and Powers, 226

'E was warned agin 'er, 201

Fair is our lot – O goodly is our heritage!, 76
'Farewell, Romance!' the Cave-men said, 150
Father, Mother, and Me, 289
For all we have and are, 132
For things we never mention, 40
Full thirty foot she towered from waterline to rail, 134

God gave all men all earth to love, 89
God of our fathers, known of old, 130

Hear now the Song of the Dead – in the North by the torn berg-edges, 78
He that hath a Gospel, 292

He wandered down the mountain grade, 282
Here come I to my own again, 259
Here we go in a flung festoon, 244

I am the land of their fathers, 227
If I have given you delight, 302
If you can keep your head when all about you, 257
If you wake at midnight, and hear a horse's feet, 276
I'm 'ere in a ticky ulster an' a broken billycock 'at, 181
In a land that the sand overlays – the ways to her gates are untrod, 123
In the Name of the Empress of India, make way, 11
In the Neolithic Age savage warfare did I wage, 143
It was not part of their blood, 281
I've a head like a concertina, I've a tongue like a button-stick, 164
I've taken my fun where I've found it, 193
I went into a public-'ouse to get a pint o' beer, 160

Kabul town's by Kabul river –, 177

Land of our Birth, we pledge to thee, 255
Let us admit it fairly, as a business people should, 114
'*Let us now praise famous men*', 249
Lord, Thou hast made this world below the shadow of a dream, 58
Love and Death once ceased their strife, 149

March! The mud is cakin' good about our trousies, 184
Master, this is Thy Servant. He is rising eight weeks old, 299
Me that 'ave been what I've been, 212
Mine was the woman to me, darkling I found her, 67
My new-cut ashlar takes the light, 235
'My son,' said the Norman Baron, 'I am dying, and you will be heir, 283

No doubt but ye are the People – your throne is above the King's, 116
No hope, no change! The clouds have shut us in, 29
Now the New Year reviving old desires, 69

Now this is the Law of the Jungle – as old and as true as the sky, 252
Oh, East is East, and West is West, and never the twain shall meet, 99
Oh, gallant was our galley from her carven steering-wheel, 24
Old Mother Laidinwool had nigh twelve months been dead, 262
One from the ends of the earth – gifts at an open door, 81
Open the old cigar-box, get me a Cuba stout, 15
Our brows are bound with spindrift and the weed is on our knees, 77

Peace is declared, an' I return, 223

Queen Bess was Harry's daughter. Stand forward partners all, 274

Rome never looks where she treads, 246
Royal and Dower-royal, I the Queen, 81

See you the ferny ride that steals, 228
Smells are surer than sounds or sights, 219
So here's your Empire. No more wine, then? Good, 18
Speakin' in general, I 'ave tried 'em all, 34

Take of English earth as much, 231
Take up the White Man's burden, 128
The bachelor 'e fights for one, 217
The Celt in all his variants from Builth to Ballyhoo, 241
The Doorkeepers of Zion, 36
The 'eathen in 'is blindness bows down to wood an' stone, 203
The Garden called Gethsemane, 43
The gull shall whistle in his wake, the blind wave break in fire, 248
The Injian Ocean sets an' smiles, 208
The men that fought at Minden, they was rookies in their time, 189
The merry clerks of Oxenford they stretch themselves at ease, 297
There are whose study is of smells, 261
There dwells a wife by the Northern Gate, 38
There's a little red-faced man, 155
There's a whisper down the field where the year has shot her yield, 72
There was a row in Silver Street that's near to Dublin Quay, 171

There was no one like 'im, 'Orse or Foot, 199
There was Rundle, Station Master, 196
The smoke upon your Altar dies, 31
The Sons of Mary seldom bother, for they have inherited that good part, 152
The wrecks dissolve above us; their dust drops down from afar, 80
They shut the road through the woods, 230
This is our lot if we live so long and labour unto the end, 126
This is the Ballad of Boh Da Thone, 104
This is the midnight – let no star, 301
To the legion of the lost ones, to the cohort of the damned, 179
Troopin', troopin', troopin' to the sea, 175
Truly ye come of The Blood; slower to bless than to ban, 84

We have no heart for the fishing – we have no hand for the oar, 120
We pulled for you when the wind was against us and the sails were low, 280
We're foot – slog – slog – slog – sloggin' over Africa, 215
We've fought with many men acrost the seas, 162
We've got the cholerer in camp – it's worse than forty fights, 191
We've sent our little Cupids all ashore, 65
We were taken from the ore-bed and the mine, 285
'What are the bugles blowin' for?' said Files-on-Parade, 158
What is a woman that you forsake her, 239
'What's that that hirples at my side?', 278
When by the labour of my 'ands, 221
When Earth's last picture is painted and the tubes are twisted and dried, 98
When Julius Fabricius, Sub-Prefect of the Weald, 264
When 'Omer smote 'is bloomin' lyre, 145
When the cabin port-holes are dark and green, 267
When the flush of a new-born sun fell first on Eden's green and gold, 141
When the Himalayan peasant meets the he-bear in his pride, 146
When you've shouted 'Rule Britannia', when you've sung 'God save the Queen', 210

Where the sober-coloured cultivator smiles, 26
Who gives him the Bath?, 237
Who hath desired the Sea? – the sight of salt water unbounded, 48
Who knows the heart of the Christian? How does he reason?, 242
Winds of the World, give answer! They are whimpering to and fro –, 95
With us there rade a Maister-Cook that came, 287

You call yourself a man, 206
You couldn't pack a Broadwood half a mile, 44
You may talk o' gin and beer, 166

MORE ABOUT PENGUINS AND PELICANS

PENGUIN MODERN POETS

1 Lawrence Durrell Elizabeth Jennings R. S. Thomas

2 Kingsley Amis Dom Moraes Peter Porter

3 George Barker Martin Bell Charles Causley

4 David Holbrook Christopher Middleton David Wevill

5 Gregory Corso Lawrence Ferlinghetti Allen Ginsberg

6 George MacBeth Edward Lucie-Smith Jack Clemo

7 Richard Murphy Jon Silkin Nathaniel Tarn

8 Edwin Brock Geoffrey Hill Stevie Smith

9 Denise Levertov Kenneth Rexroth William Carlos Williams

10 Adrian Henri Roger McGough Brian Patten

11 D. M. Black Peter Redgrove D. M. Thomas

12 Alan Jackson Jeff Nuttall William Wantling

13 Charles Bukowski Philip Lamantia Harold Norse

14 Alan Brownjohn Michael Hamburger Charles Tomlinson

15 Alan Bold Edward Brathwaite Edwin Morgan

16 Jack Beeching Harry Guest Matthew Mead

17 W. S. Graham Kathleen Raine David Gascoyne

18 A. Alvarez Roy Fuller Anthony Thwaite

19 John Ashbery Lee Harwood Tom Raworth

20 John Heath-Stubbs F. T. Prince Stephen Spender

21 George Mackay Brown Norman MacCaig Iain Crichton Smith

22 John Fuller Peter Levi Adrian Mitchell

23 Geoffrey Grigson Edwin Muir Adrian Stokes

24 Kenward Elmslie Kenneth Koch James Schuyler

25 Gavin Ewart Zulfikar Ghose B. S. Johnson

POET TO POET

In the introductions to their personal selections from work of poets they have admired, the individual editors write as follows:

CRABBE SELECTED BY C. DAY LEWIS

'As his poetry displays a balance and decorum in its versification, so his moral ideal is a kind of normality to which every civilized being should aspire. This, when one looks at the desperate expedients and experiments of poets (and others) today, is at least refreshing.'

HENRYSON SELECTED BY HUGH MACDIARMID

'There is now a consensus of judgement that regards Henryson as the greatest of our great makars. Literary historians and other commentators in the bad period of the century preceding the twenties of our own century were wont to group together as the great five: Henryson, Dunbar, Douglas, Lyndsay, and King James I; but in the critical atmosphere prevailing today it is clear that Henryson (who was, with the exception of King James, the youngest of them) is the greatest.'

HERBERT SELECTED BY W. H. AUDEN

'The two English poets, neither of them, perhaps, major poets, whom I would most like to have known well are William Barnes and George Herbert.

Even if Isaac Walton had never written his life, I think that any reader of his poetry will conclude that George Herbert must have been an exceptionally good man, and exceptionally nice as well.'

Further selections include the work of Cotton, Ben Jonson, Pope *and* Shelley.

A Pelican Biography

RUDYARD KIPLING

His Life and Work

Charles Carrington

'It is one of the virtues of Carrington's admirable biography that through the care and sobriety of his narrative we catch the pulse of the legend . . . A very good biography – we are not left, as we so often are when we have closed an official life, with the thought "here is a quarry where other men in the future may dig more profitably". Mr Carrington has dug with effect. The quarry is closed' – Graham Greene in the *London Magazine*.

'A genuine portrait which can be recommended not only to lovers of Kipling but to every student of human nature . . . sound, scholarly, yet never for a moment dull' – Peter Quennell in the *Daily Mail*.

'For the present, this is the indispensable source-book for Kipling scholars . . . there is, incidentally, some criticism independent of current fashion and well worth attending to' – Pamela Hansford Johnson in the *Bookman*.

'The only complaint is that the book, though five hundred pages long, is fifty pages short . . . we want more' – *The Times Literary Supplement*

RUDYARD KIPLING

Short Stories, volumes 1 and 2:

A Sahib's War and Other Stories

Friendly Brook and Other Stories

Edited by Andrew Rutherford

Of the two volumes, *A Sahib's War and Other Stories* and *Friendly Brook and Other Stories*, Professor Rutherford, who selected the contents of both volumes, writes: 'There are fewer tales of Empire than the popular stereotype of Kipling might lead readers to expect. . . . Increasingly he was preoccupied by the condition of England herself, as he rebuked her blindness, folly and complacency, and sought reassurance in groups, types or individuals who might still redeem her backslidings. Simultaneously, he found himself involved in a fascinating process of discovery, for the country-side, its people and traditions, came as a revelation to him once he settled in Sussex . . . Public themes bulk large in *A Sahib's War and Other Stories*, as his preoccupation with the Great War does in *Friendly Brook and Other Stories*; but these coexist with more personal, psychological, and more spiritual interests, especially in his later years . . . using a remarkable variety of settings and of *dramatis personae*, he offers stories on a characteristic range of themes – stories of revenge, seen sometimes as wild justice, sometimes as an almost pathological obsession: stories of forgiveness, human and divine; stories of the supernatural, to be taken now literally, now symbolically, but never trivially as mere spine-chilling entertainment; stories of hatred and cruelty, but stories also of compassion and of love; stories of work, of craftsmanship, of artistry; of comradeship and isolation; and stories of healing, sometimes physical, but more often moral, spiritual or psychological.'